DUBLIN
AND HER PEOPLE

CLB 1708
© 1987 Colour Library Books Ltd., Guildford, Surrey, England.
Printed and bound in Barcelona, Spain by Cronion, S.A.
All rights reserved.
1987 edition published by Crescent Books, distributed by Crown Publishers, Inc.
ISBN 0 517 62362 5
h g f e d c b a

DUBLIN
AND HER PEOPLE

Matthew Byrne

CRESCENT BOOKS
NEW YORK

STAND ANYWHERE IN O'CONNELL STREET,
and the one thing you're aware of is people.
But that's not surprising.
Dublin is people. Hasting, shuffling, rushing,
bustling, dreaming, scheming, sobbing, sighing, laughing,
singing, talking, seldom listening.
Then there are the ones that don't move.
They stand
in monumental line down the middle of O'Connell Street,
each with his back turned resolutely on the other.

Parnell on perpetual point-duty at the top. Past Father Mathew with the Capuchin habit he never had in life. Sir John Gray, whose water supply has been known to dilute many a glass of whiskey, and William Smith O'Brien. And pleading Jim Larkin, his arms outstretched to Dan O'Connell with his angels at the bottom. They're Dublin, too. The pop-ups that spring from the pages of the history book, a reminder that history in Dublin is no more than a man's attempt at telling some of the story of Dublin's people.

If you're standing anywhere near O'Connell Bridge, you're by the River Liffey on whose banks the story began once upon a time.

It's hard to be precise about the date of the city's foundation.

It's not easy to be exact about the place, either. Dublin is known in Gaelic by two names – Ath Cliath, the Ford of the Hurdles; and Dubh Linn, the Black Pool.

Was it two different places, more or less in the same area? Was it one place with two names?

The Black Pool, formed by the confluence of the Liffey and the River Poddle, was what attracted the Vikings who played so big a part in establishing Dublin.

They had been coming and going along the east coast for about forty years. Eventually, in the summer of 837, they decided to stay at Dyfflin, as they called it.

They stayed because they liked it. It was convenient. Not only for safe anchorage, but as a good base from which to increase their forays into Europe. To say nothing of the clearway it gave them to the gold in the Wicklow hills.

Ath Cliath was pre-Viking. It was a ford, constructed of stone and wooden beams, across the Liffey. Ath Cliath sat at the cross-roads of Ireland – the Sli Mhór from the west; the Sli Midhluarchara (the road through the

marshes) from the north; the Sli Dála (the road of meetings) from the south.

Sited where Fr. Mathew Bridge is now, the Hurdle Ford was Dublin's bridge. It provided an obvious and necessary access from the north side of the wide, shallow and dangerously tidal Liffey to a centre of population on the south bank.

And this centre of population, certainly from the time Christianity gained hold in Ireland, seems to have developed into a sizable town, if the number of pre-Viking churches in the area is anything to go by.

St. Audoen's, which dates from the twelfth century, replaced the ancient St. Columcille's, built before the Vikings. St. Werburgh's was built alongside a site once occupied by the Church of St. Martin. St. Bride (or St. Brigid) and St. Kevin also had churches dedicated to them. Their names, if not their churches, are still remembered in the area where once the River Poddle flowed freely, but now runs underground.

Building present-day St. Patrick's Cathedral began in 1192. But back in 450 there was already a church on the site, an island, in fact, between two branches of the River Poddle.

St. Patrick himself is said to have baptised converts on the site. Legend has it that he caused a holy well to spring forth to provide water for the baptism... an act that looks a little ostentatious with the Poddle all round him. The well, though, was still going strong in the Middle Ages, and was said to have great healing properties.

Wells were something of a trade-mark with the Saint in Dublin. Besides the one at St. Patrick's Cathedral, he is credited with two others. One in the Provost's Garden in Trinity College. The other in Nassau Place that earned Nassau Street the name St. Patrick's Well Lane for long enough, and made its own contribution to the city's water supply.

St. Patrick, however, knew nothing of that, for he was long gone by then, and his identification, if not his very existence, a matter for discussion amongst the academics.

In the meantime, the Vikings, if they didn't actually found the city of Dublin, certainly worked hard in establishing it.

When they came ashore as settlers in their flat-bottomed boats, they staked their claim in the shape of a twelve-foot-high stone pillar, set up on the sandy beach, not far from where the Dodder and the Liffey joined the sea.

The standing stone was called the Steyne (Steine or Staine) and gave its name to a whole district – the Steyne of Dublin. It stood for almost eight hundred years, a silent watcher as time and people brought changes to the waterlogged land around it.

It witnessed All Hallows Priory, that Dermott Mac Murrough built, stand and flourish with the tide still lapping close. In the Middle Ages, pilgrims on their way to Rome and England rested at the nearby Hospice which Henry de Loundres founded for them. And westward, beyond the Priory, where the land was green, sheep and cattle grazed, beggars camped, and citizens made holiday or watched a hanging at the public gallows.

In 1327 it stood in the trails of smoke from the fire at Hoggen Green when Adam O'Toole of Leinster was burnt at the stake for heresy. There were no half-measures about the man. And nothing mealy-mouthed about his opinions that contradicted everything that those in the Nunnery nearby or at the Priory stood for. He denied the divinity of Jesus; the Bible he considered a fable; and the Blessed Virgin, he reckoned, was a woman of dissolute habit.

Two hundred years later, the Priory itself was left a dereliction, when Henry VIII dissolved All Hallows in his move against the monasteries.

And spare stood the land near the now ancient Steyne till Elizabeth I, in 1591, granted the charter to establish Trinity College.

The overflowing Liffey sometimes washed the College's north wall. Till 1663, when William Hawkins built his wall to stop the Liffey's tidal effect, and began the reclamation of the land on the south side of the river.

Hawkins paved the way for Burgh Quay, and got a street named after him.

Whether by accident or design, nobody can be sure, but a few years after Hawkins' wall was built, the Steyne disappeared. The junction of Townsend Street and Hawkins' Street marks the spot where it stood.

As quietly as the old stone disappeared, however, a new one appeared two hundred and fifty years later. In March 1986 the Corporation erected Cliodhna Cussen's granite sculpture, looking as much as posssible like the original steyne.

The reception the Vikings got in Dublin was hardly heart warming. But they were strong enough, and had enough battle experience to impress themselves on their reluctant hosts.

They built their fortress where Dublin Castle stands today. And developed the area round the fortress – Christ Church Place, Winetavern Street and Fishamble Street.

We can form some idea of their daily life and occupations from the collection in the National Museum. Some of the collection comes from excavations in the 1960s round High Street and Christ Church Place. They were fine craftsmen in wood, metal and leather. They fished and hunted, built and repaired boats. They learnt and spoke Gaelic, and adopted the Christianity of the local people. Even the coins they minted bore a cross on one side, and the head of Sitric, the Danish king of Dublin, on the other. It is said, though, that the men rarely carried coins. On the odd occasion when they did, they wrapped them in a rag, or stuck them with beeswax under their armpits.

Of course, they married Irish women.

King Sitric himself married Brian Boru's daughter, Saidhbh. And history might have assumed they lived happily ever after had it not been for the battle of Clontarf.

It was Good Friday, April 23, 1014. Sitric and his queen stood looking over the parapet of their fortress in Dublin.

The fires still smouldered in the outlying districts that Brian Boru had systematically set alight since his arrival, on March 17, in the area we now call Kilmainham and the Phoenix Park.

Now the Danes, and Brian Boru's Irishmen, supported by some of their Scots relatives, were ranged and ready for battle.

From where they stood, Sitric and his wife could see the battle-ground. It stretched from today's O'Connell Bridge to the River Tolka and out towards Clontarf. The bitterest fighting was round the fishing weir of the Tolka, near the present Ballybough Bridge.

From this distance, it was difficult for Sitric to see everything in precise detail.

It was late afternoon by now. The battle had raged from early morning. It looked to Sitric as though things were going well for the Danes. There was a natural tinge of triumph in his voice as he spoke to his queen. "Well do the foreigners reap the field," he said. "See how they fling the sheaves to the ground."

It was a thoughtless kind of remark. For, after all, his wife's seventy-three-year-old father was down there, and her brothers, cousins, and her fifteen-year-old nephew Turlough. Sitric might have been in the slaughter himself had he not been left to guard the city.

Who loomed largest in her thoughts, however, Saidhbh did not reveal. And her voice was quiet as she spoke, counselling caution. "The result will be seen at the close of the day," she said.

And they watched.

Till towards the evening.

Then the Irish made an all-out attack.

The Danes fled. All out along the level shore towards Dublin, hoping to get to safety in the city by the only bridge across the Liffey, or reach their ships at anchor in the Bay.

They were caught between the Irish and the sea. Those who weren't killed by the sword were being forced into the sea to drown.

Sitric and his wife saw it all.

"It seems to me," remarked Saidhbh to Sitric, "that the foreigners are making fast for their inheritance – the sea."

Sitric was listening.

And his wife continued. "They look like a herd of cows galloping over the plain on a sultry summer day, driven mad by heat and gadflies..."

Sitric still listened, but did not look best pleased. And his wife might have been wise to notice the signs.

She wasn't.

She went on, "But indeed, they do not look like cows that wait to be milked."

Sitric was angry. He might have reacted differently had he known that his father-in-law was amongst the slain.

But he didn't.

He lashed out wildly at his wife, hit her on the mouth, and broke one of her teeth.

History does not reveal how they patched things up. History does, however, make clear that the Viking power in Ireland was finished, and its kingdom contained in Dublin.

In their own way, the settlers left their mark on Dublin. They left behind St. Mary's Abbey, St. Michan's, and the beginnings of Christ Church Cathedral. And, unawares, provided stones to repair Dublin's boundary wall in the 1300s, and the building of Essex Bridge. And enough in-fill to solve a flooding problem at St. Patrick's Well Lane in 1682.

Dealing with the flooding was not, of course, the prime concern at the time. The important matter was moving a massive mound of earth as part of a redevelopment programme by Sir William Davis, Chief Justice of Ireland.

The mound was a legacy from the Vikings. It was their Thingmound or Thingmote, a forty-foot-high mound used as a meeting place where they enacted laws and dispensed justice. Situated in today's Suffolk Street, roughly where St. Andrew's Church is, its massive size protected it for almost seven hundred years.

When Sir William decided it had to go, the earth was used to fill in nearby St. Patrick's Well Lane which had, for years, suffered from flooding.

The effect of the work is apparent even today. There's no longer a mound, of course. But Nassau Street, as the Lane was later named, is about ten feet above the level of College Park, the playing fields of Trinity College.

St. Mary's Abbey, on the north side of the river, is said to be the first Danish foundation in Dublin. It was built outside the city walls.

In its time it housed Benedictine monks and then the Cistercians. To say nothing of the Viceroys when they were not using Thomas Court or the Palace of St. Sepulchre near St. Patrick's Cathedral.

By the end of the twelfth century, it was one of the richest religious houses in Dublin. Besides owning five thousand acres on the north side of the river, it had an estate that stretched from Blackrock to Dunlaoghaire. The area is still known as Monkstown. With exclusive salmon rights on the Liffey, it ran a fishing business from its own harbour at the mouth of the River Bradoge, in the days before the quays were built along the Liffey. The harbour was known as The Pill, and gave its name to Pill Lane which, today, is called Chancery Street.

It suffered a fire in 1304. Shortly after that, its tower was demolished to provide some of the stones to strengthen the city's fortifications.

The Abbey itself went the way of a good many religious houses in Henry VIII's dissolution of the monasteries. It was a dereliction by the time Sir Humphrey Jervis bought it and its twenty acres for redevelopment. As part of his plan, he built Essex Bridge, using stones from St. Mary's Abbey.

All that remains, now, of the Abbey is the Chapter House in Meeting House Lane.

The Chapter House hides away, enmeshed in the bustle of the fruit and vegetable market on one side, and traffic-snarled Capel Street on the other. It stands beside a bedding factory, and is embodied in a building that was once a seed-merchant's warehouse.

A notice on the door advises that the key is obtainable from Mrs. Coleman at 4A Ormonde Square. Mrs. Coleman, it must be reported, has left 4A. But a kind neighbour, wreathed in cigarette smoke and sounding Scottish, directed me across to Mrs. Tyrrell at No. 35. And there I got the key from her young and mannerly nephew Justin.

The floor of the Chapter House is about eight feet below

present street level. Which, as the man said, "only proves how much Dublin has come up in the world since them days."

And some days they were, if June 11th, 1534 is anything to go by.

It was St. Barnabas' Day. And the day Lord Thomas Fitzgerald, with his retinue of one-hundred-and-forty, rode to St. Mary's Abbey and stormed into the Chapter House to renounce his allegiance to Henry VIII.

His father, Garrett Og, ninth Earl of Kildare, was Lord Deputy of Ireland, appointed by Henry VIII. The Fitzgeralds had a reputation as fighters. Garrett ruled like a king. His enemies gave a sinister twist to his attempts at government in their reports to the king. Maybe he had rebellion in mind. He certainly furnished his castles with guns, pikes and gunpowder from the stores in Dublin Castle.

A peremptory summons from Henry brought him to London to give an account of his stewardship.

He left his son in charge of the Council.

Twenty years old and with the nickname 'Silken' from the silk trappings he and his retinue wore, Thomas may not have been the best choice.

Judging from the speech the old earl made in appointing his son, it looks as though he himself had some misgivings.

But Silken Thomas was in charge.

The enemies worked hard, and eventually convinced the young man that his father had been executed in London.

Silken Thomas reacted. In the Chapter House.

Storming in, he threw the Sword of State and his robes of office on the table, renouncing his allegiance to the king.

Archbishop Cromer, whom his father had appointed Lord Chancellor, tried to dissuade him. The Council tried. The very Council of whom his father had told him, "that for wisdom is able to lesson you with sound and sage advice."

They might have succeeded had a bard and some others in the Chapter House not encouraged him to avenge his father's death.

His business completed, Silken Thomas rode off with his one-hundred-and-forty men to attack Dublin Castle. The attack failed. He was chased out of Dublin, and took refuge in his castle at Maynooth.

The summer and winter passed while Sir William Skeffington, whom Henry had appointed Deputy, recovered from sickness. Then he besieged Thomas in Maynooth. The castle was battered with artillery – the first time artillery was seriously used in Ireland.

Silken Thomas eventually surrendered, having been promised that his life would be spared.

It was. For eighteen months which he had to spend languishing in the Tower of London, till he was executed with his five uncles at Tyburn.

Turn right out of Meeting House Lane. Along Chancery Street, past the Dublin City Markets. Across Arran Street. Then a right incline across the traffic at Church Street. And there it is. The church that, for six hundred years, was the only parish church on the north side of the Liffey. St. Michan's.

Who precisely St. Michan was is anybody's guess. The general view is that he was a Danish saint. Some, though, declare he was a Dublin man, a martyr and confessor. Whoever he was, he is the saint to whom the church King Sitric founded was dedicated on May 14, 1095.

St. Michan's is the oldest building on the north side of the Liffey. Were it not for Christ Church Cathedral, it would be the oldest in the entire city. Christ Church has that distinction by a few years. St. Michan's did not have to suffer the hazards Christ Church had to bear. And it escaped the fate Sir Humphrey Jervis meted out to St. Mary's Abbey.

By the time Jervis began opening up the area, St. Michan's was in a poor state. But Jervis didn't pull it down. Instead, St. Michan's was repaired. It was virtually rebuilt under its rector Dr. John Pooley in 1686. The tower with its battlements remained. Parts of the original church building itself remained, and the foundations are, almost certainly, original.

Today's church is a remodelled St. Michan's.

The Parish Beadle's seat is there in the gallery, near the organ. In 1724 they paid eight pounds for the carving on the front of the gallery. It is a carving of seventeen musical instruments. All from one block of wood. At the West end are the recessed pews for the church wardens and the judges from the nearby Four Courts. At the East end, they keep the only eighteenth-century Chair of Repentance in Dublin. It was used. As Christopher Pell, if he were alive today, could tell.

Mr. Pell had a row with the clergy over the funeral of his child. He was summoned before the Archbishop of Dublin to explain his conduct. As a punishment, he was sentenced to do public penance in St. Michan's.

Thirty minutes before the start of the morning service, Christopher Pell stood in St. Michan's porch. Barefooted, dressed only in a long white shift, he implored the prayers of each worshipper arriving to join the congregation.

The service began. Pell still stood. And waited till the end of the second Lesson, when the minister approached to conduct him to the Chair of Repentance.

The minister led. Pell followed. And all along the aisle the minister intoned the penitential fifty-first psalm, whose verses left Christopher Pell in no doubt about his miserable state.

The psalm was finished by the time they reached the Chair of Repentance, placed carefully near the lofty pulpit. Pell mounted the steps, to stand in what itself looked like a miniature pulpit.

Faces stared up at him from the ground floor, and all round him from the gallery.

And they listened to the sermon that measured the gravity of Christopher's offence.

Chastened as he was now, and sufficiently shamed in the eyes of all that had not the same need or opportunity to transgress, Christopher Pell confessed his offence, and offered a prayer for forgiveness.

And joined the congregation then, as they took their lead from the minister and recited the Creed.

Rumour has it that Handel played the organ at St. Michan's during his extended visit to Dublin for the premiere of The Messiah in 1742.

The rumour could well be true. In 1742, the organ at St. Michan's was the most important in Dublin, and St. Michan's itself the most fashionable church in the city. Whether or aye, the console he is reputed to have used is on view in the south porch.

Thirteen years before Handel's visit, Edmund Burke, who was born in 1729, around the corner at No. 12 Arran Quay, was baptised there. Henry Jackson's daughter, Eleanor, who later married Oliver Bond, the secretary of the United Irishmen, was baptised in St. Michan's. Oliver Bond himself is buried in the graveyard.

And Robert Emmet. Though there is some debate about that. There is an argument that he is buried in an unmarked grave in Bully's Acre, across the road from Kilmainham Jail.

The story is that when Emmet was hanged, and beheaded with a butcher's knife, in Thomas Street on September 20, 1803, his body was brought back to Kilmainham, and buried in Bully's Acre.

St. Michan's comes into the story because of the Reverend Thomas Gamble, one of St. Michan's clergy. Thomas Gamble ministered to Robert Emmet on the scaffold. A week after the execution, it is said, Mr. Gamble claimed the young patriot's body, and had it taken from Bully's Acre and buried in St. Michan's churchyard.

But were the church never involved with the history and people of the city, it would still be famous for its vaults, where the bodies and coffins, after hundreds of years, are still in a wonderful state of preservation.

Why it is so has not yet been satisfactorily explained. It has been suggested that it is because it is built on limestone rock which has a peculiar drying effect. The temperature in the vaults is a constant 52°F.

It may, however, be the relatively high methane content in the air of the vaults which acts as a preservative, as A.T. Lucas, director of the National Museum, suggested in 1964.

Whatever it is, the bodies are preserved. With skin like leather. Amongst them, 'The Crusader' as he is known. A man about seven feet tall, his legs were broken to fit him into the coffin. Legend has it that whoever shakes his hand will have good luck. And judging from his well polished, leather-brown hand, The Crusader has brought luck to countless thousands.

Maybe he brought luck to Dubliner Bram Stoker, visiting the vaults from his house in Harcourt Street. They say it was a visit to the vaults that inspired Stoker to write some of his book 'Dracula'.

The Sheares Brothers are buried in the vaults. But their coffins are not preserved. They were, once. But on the centenary of their execution, some well-meaning people, marking the anniversary, brought fresh flowers in a vase. The coffins rotted. The decomposition, they say, caused by bacteria in either the flowers or the water. The bodies were recoffined. But, from then on, fresh flowers were banned from the vaults.

The Sheares Brothers, John and Henry, were young barristers involved in plotting the rebellion of 1798.

Betrayed by a man named Armstrong, they were arrested on May 21, two days before the rebellion was timed to begin. They were convicted on July 12, and were hanged at Newgate prison two days later.

Five minutes after the execution, the notice arrived of a reprieve for Henry Sheares.

The prison at the time was just on ten years completed. 'New' Newgate as it was called, it replaced the Newgate in Cornmarket, near Christ Church. The 'new' Newgate was built in Little Green Street, by Green Street Courthouse, and about ten minutes' walk from St. Michan's. It boasted sophisticated machinery in its new gallows room – a windlass for raising and lowering the bodies of criminals after they were executed.

It was demolished in 1893.

Today the site is marked by a memorial in a park that provides a playground with a handball alley.

And sometimes children play there, and the noise of their excited innocence makes strange sound in the sad silence that seems, nowadays, to be the abiding atmosphere round Green Street Courthouse. Halston Street and Green Street are normally cordoned by security barriers. Not many people walk there now. And the barriers are moved only to make way for armed convoys bringing political prisoners to Green Street for trial.

A far cry from the days when Little Green Street

reflected the patch of greenery before the prison was ever built. And the River Bradoge flowed, and Halston Street was better known as Halfstone Street. When Jervis Street was still unheard of, and they knew the area as Trepois Park, and Abbey Street as The Black Wardrobe, and nobody ever imagined that Ash Park could be transformed into Upper O'Connell Street. And an even farther cry from the long-gone days of 1189, when Little John from England's Sherwood Forest stood on the only bridge across the Liffey. And shot an arrow as far as Oxmantown Green – the length of present-day Church Street – just to show how good he was.

A clever archer was Robin Hood's enormous lieutenant. But not clever enough, if the story is correct, to avoid being hanged in the fields of Oxmantown, near the spot where a later generation erected the building in Blackhall Place which now houses the Incorporated Law Society of Ireland.

Up to 1970, the building belonged to The King's Hospital, or The Blue Coat School, as it was called for long enough. It got its name because of the long, blue, cassock-like coats the boys wore.

The school was founded in 1669, with a charter from Charles II. To this day, its title preserves the name of the ancient district in which it was built – The Hospital and Free School of King Charles II, Oxmantown.

When the school began, its premises were in Queen Street. A new building was begun in Blackhall Place in 1773, and the school moved there.

Both buildings were, in fact, on Oxmantown Green. The school playing field was the last surviving part of Oxmantown Green.

The King's Hospital, like other schools facing the economics of education in the city, decided to move. Alexandra College, Wesley College, and the High School made the same decision.

The King's Hospital moved in 1970, to newly-built premises in Palmerstown, beyond Phoenix Park, on the Lucan Road. The Blackhall Place building was bought by the Incorporated Law Society of Ireland. They did a magnificent restoration job on it. And they, like the building's first owners, retained the one bit of Oxmanton left in the city.

The lawyers who lunch there are no more than a comfortable stroll away from their Law Courts.

The Four Courts, as the building is called, is a grand reminder of an age of elegance in Dublin's history. But pock-marked grandeur that tells, too, of Dublin's sadness, scored and scarred as it is by the shells and bullets of the Civil War of 1922.

It is one of James Gandon's masterpieces. That Englishman of taste and perseverance who arrived in Dublin to fulfil a commission. Like many an immigrant before and since, he stayed and made his home for more than forty years amongst the people of Dublin. And at the age of eighty was buried amongst them in Drumcondra.

James Gandon was a pupil of Sir William Chambers, the architect of Somerset House in London.

He came to Dublin at the invitation of Sir John Beresford, despite Princess Dashkov's attempts at luring him to Russia to work for Catherine the Great. Though the Princess might, in fact, have been easier to resist than Sir John. Beresford was a powerful and obstinate man. He was Commissioner of Revenue, and ruled like a king in Ireland. He found it difficult to be happy with 'no' as an answer.

He had made up his mind to build a new Custom House further down the Liffey. And Gandon would be the architect.

Beresford himself laid the foundation-stone of the Custom House on August 8, 1781, almost in secret.

The foundation-stone of the Four Courts, in contrast, was laid on March 13, 1786, with great pomp and circumstance. The Duke of Rutland performed the ceremony, with the Lord Chancellor, Lord Lifford, and all the judiciary attending in full state.

Ten years later, and at a cost of £200,000, the building was completed. On a site that for almost two-hundred-and-fifty years already had been associated, one way or another, with the law.

The Dominicans had lived happily enough on the site for several hundred years.

Until 1539.

Then, following the suppressiom of the monasteries by Henry VIII, their priory was taken over, first as lodgings for the lawyers, and then as courts. Even James II had his Patriot Parliament there in 1689. And he might have benefitted from some legal advice on the mint he established a bit further down the Liffey, at 27 Capel Street.

It was the first mint in Ireland. But the coins it produced from pots and pans, cannon-balls and broken bells could hardly be described as legal tender. Though traders who refused to accept the coinage risked being hanged.

The crazy money seemed to suit the bedlam state of the city during James' stay there, from the time he arrived on Palm Sunday, March 24, 1689, till his hasty departure in July 1690.

The day before he left, he had led an army to the River Boyne against William of Orange. His army defeated, James led the retreat of his exhausted men. Lady Tyrconnell, it is said, met him at Dublin Castle. The king commented sourly that the cowardly Irish had run away from the battle. To which Lady Tyrconnell offered, "It seems that your majesty won the race."

Next morning James had left Dublin, going, via Bray and

Waterford, to France.

The Dominicans, who had long occupied the Four Courts site, collected tolls from the travellers on the bridge nearby which King John had built in 1210.

King John did it to replace the bridge at the Ford of the Hurdles. The Dominicans, in their turn, rebuilt King John's 'Dublin Bridge' in 1385. It was called Friars Bridge for long enough. And then The Old Bridge.

In a city that seems to have spent a good deal of its time renaming bridges, this bridge must be the most renamed.

It was completely rebuilt in 1816 as Whitworth Bridge. It became known as Church Street Bridge. Nowadays it's called Father Mathew Bridge, in memory of Fr. Theobold Mathew who, in 1840, began a fierce campaign against drinking and drunkeness.

His campaign had effect. On both sides. It is reckoned that by the end of 1840, some one-hundred-thousand people had signed the pledge to abstain from alcohol. And some brewers went bankrupt.

But there is a kind of humour in the present name of the bridge. It is dedicated to the apostle of temperance. It crosses the Liffey, whose waters are purported to give Guinness its unique taste. And it leads from Church Street to Bridge Street and the oldest pub in Dublin, the Brazen Head Inn. To say nothing of being within staggering distance of Winetavern Street.

It may be some kind of residual influence of Fr. Mathew that has the effect of damping all thoughts of drinking, and delays the visit to the Brazen Head. It may, of course, be that the eye is distracted by the obelisk that dominates the skyline in the west.

Whatever it is, while one half of the mind argues the nice difference between temperance and total abstinence, the other half can travel the few miles from the bridge to the Phoenix Park where the obelisk is.

The journey is along the south bank of the river. By Usher's Quay and Usher's Island. Past the remnants of Moira House, and The Sick and Indigent Roomkeepers Institute or 'The Sick and Indignant' as Dubliners call it. The building is gone, but the charity remains, and still does its good work.

Across Watling Street, then, to stand and stare awhile on Victoria Quay.

Running the whole length of Victoria Quay is the St. James's Gate Brewery – Guinness'. Not so long ago, the barrels of stout and porter were trundled across the road on miniature railways to be loaded onto barges at the wooden wharves that lined the quay. The barges sailed down the Liffey to load them onto the Guinness' boats for export. The wharves are gone now. And the barges. Nowadays, the porter travels down the quays to the boats in container lorries.

On the opposite bank of the river, what began as a military post behind the Blue Coat School on Oxmantown Green, by 1701 had become the Royal Barracks.

In the meantime, the military decided a bridge was needed to replace the ferry-boat service across the river. The builders began the wooden structure that would be known as Barrack Bridge.

The ferrymen objected. They were supported by the apprentices. And together they attacked the soldiers in an attempt to put a stop to the building.

The ferrymen lost. In bloodshed. The bridge, for many a long year, was called Bloody Bridge. Replaced later, it was named Victoria Bridge. Nowadays it's called Watling Street Bridge.

The Royal Barracks is Collins' Barracks now, and the Barrack Street that ran outside it is renamed Benburb Street.

There's a playing-field not much bigger than a football pitch between the barracks and the river. It runs along Sarsfield Quay. Behind the railings is a standing stone, inscribed "1798". It marks the grave of the United Irishmen who took part in the rebellion of 1798. Flogged, tortured, hanged, and some of them beheaded, their bodies were thrown into the mass grave prepared on what was then a patch of waste ground between the river and the barracks. It's known, now, as The Croppies' Hole.

Almost fifty years later, the same patch of ground was trampled by thousands of starving men, women and children struggling their way to the soup kitchen at the Royal Barracks.

It was authority's attempt at helping the victims of the Famine in 1847.

The potato blight hit Ireland in 1845. The effect, though, was not seriously felt in Dublin till the winter of 1846, when the resources of the city could no longer deal with the thousands of refugees that flooded into the city from all parts of Ireland.

In January 1847 Parliament passed 'The Soup Kitchen Act.' Under it, government and charities collaborated to try to alleviate the utter devastation. A Model Soup Kitchen was set-up outside the Royal Barracks, and people queued in their thousands, day after day, to be fed. They were allowed in, one hundred at a time, for a bowl of soup specially concocted by Alexis Soyer, the master chef of the London Reform Club.

Chef he might have been, but Alexis could hardly claim to be a nutrition expert when it came to nourishing the famine victims. What he reckoned was enough to sustain a strong, healty man was, in fact, watery vegetable soup made of ox heads. It was doled out at the rate of three hundred gallons a day to over eight thousand people.

Across the road from the end of Victoria Quay stands Heuston Station which, like the bridge beside it, was first called King's Bridge.

Turning left round Guinness' wall is Steevens' Lane, which got its name from the hospital which has been there since 1733.

'Quaint' and 'picturesque' are words people use to describe its appearance. There is an air of peace and healing in the cloisters that run round the courtyard.

Richard Steevens, after whom the hospital is named, was professor of medicine at Trinity College and President of the College of Physicians.

He made a will bequeathing his estate to his spinster sister Grizel, to benefit her for life, and after her death to build a hospital.

One day the will was made. Next day Richard Steevens died. Miss Steevens decided to build the hospital without delay, the only condition being that she be allowed to have an apartment at the hospital.

The hospital was built in what was then wide-open countryside, to escape the infections of the city.

Grizel had her apartment. And regularly sat in the window to allow herself to be seen by passing Dubliners. Not out of pride and vainglory, but to scotch a notion that she wore a veil in public to hide her face that had the snout of a pig.

Being a lady, considerate Dubliners said, she always ate from a silver trough. And she had a pig's head, they said, because of a curse a beggar-woman put on her poor mother.

The beggar-woman, a baby in her arms and a litter of children in tow, it seems, accosted Mrs Steevens, imploring alms.

"Away with you," snapped Mrs. Steevens, "You and your litter of bonhams."

The beggar-woman was hurt. But not lost for words. She cursed Mrs. Steevens that her next child be like a pig.

There is a choice of bridges crossing the Liffey from Steevens' Lane to Phoenix Park.

One is Heuston Bridge. The other is Droichead Phroinsias Ui Shearbháin, built in 1984 beside it to take the traffic strain from Heuston Bridge.

Either will do.

And on either one a romantic soul might stop and, in imagination, follow the river west.

A different river, now. No longer tied and bound by granite, nor hemmed-in by city streets. But free and wandering. By Longmeadows where the grass grows multi-shaded green, and the Strawberry Beds where only the trees cast shadows.

And then a busy river, rushing in noisy gossipings at the weirs. The Wren's Nest where boy and girl canoeists test their skills, or Shackleton's Weir where the sundial tells the time and the mill turns by the river's power. And after Lucan, stillness again, and quietness to Leixlip and the Salmon Leap.

And if the Liffey has not already enough bridges in Dublin, it has more as it reaches its continuously lovely way through County Kildare to its rising in Kippure in County Wicklow...

But in the middle of a busy bridge, with traffic speeding by and travellers skirting past, manhandling their luggage to the station, the soliloquy has to end.

Across the bridge, bear left with the road, and, as Dubliners say, it's no distance to the Park.

An entrance the width of the road. The main gates are gone, demolished in 1932 for the Eucharistic Congress. The original pillars that went along with the gates were replaced in August 1986. And there, to the left of the main road through Phoenix Park, is the obelisk that first caught the eye way back on Fr. Mathew Bridge.

Compared with the Park itself, the obelisk is only a milestone in history.

Dubliners call it The Monument. It was erected to the memory of the Duke of Wellington, a Dublin man who preferred to be known as a Londoner.

He was born at 24 Lr. Merrion Street. But, as he remarked himself, being born in Dublin didn't make him Irish, any more than being born in a stable would make him a horse. For all that, though, Dublin shaped him. As a boy he went to school at Samuel Whyte's school in Grafton Street – where Bewley's Cafe is today. He spent his early manhood in the city, married his wife Catherine Sarah Packenham in St. George's, and served in Dublin as aide-de-camp to the Viceroy.

The bronze frieze round the Monument is a reminder of his ability as a soldier. The frieze is cast from the bronze of cannon taken in battle.

In his own way, he made a contribution to Irish history. In 1829. When Pitt, pushed by Daniel O'Connell and public opinion, introduced a Bill for Catholic Emancipation, it was given a rough passage in Parliament. It was the Duke who argued that the alternative to Catholic Emancipation was civil war in Ireland. The Bill was passed on April 13, 1829.

Phoenix Park is the largest city park in Europe. All one-thousand-seven-hundred-and-fifty-two acres of it. Originally, though, it was two thousand acres when James Butler, Duke of Ormonde, took it over as part of the sequestered lands of Kilmainham Priory.

He used just on two-hundred-and-fifty acres to build the Royal Hospital, Kilmainham. The rest he set aside as a deer park for the Viceroy.

The descendants of those original English deer still

roam freely in the Park, and, except in the rutting season or when the does drop their young, they are tame enough to be approached quite closely.

It is hard to decide whether or not Ormonde had posterity in mind in his work on the Park. However, he worked hard to keep the Park out of the hands of the scheming Duchess of Cleveland.

The duchess, sometimes known by her Irish title, Lady Castlemaine, was the mistress of Charles II. The papers giving the land to the duchess were already prepared. Ormonde, however, persuaded the king to change his mind. The duchess was not pleased. She was a beautiful woman, as her portrait in Dublin Castle shows. Her temper, though, did not match her appearance. And poor Ormonde felt the whiplash of her tongue as she made it clear to him that her fervent hope was to see him hanged.

He wasn't hanged, of course. He lived long enough to see the Vice-regal Lodge built, and a lodge for the Chief Secretary.

Posterity improved and enlarged both buildings. The Vice-regal Lodge became, in 1921, the home of the Governor General of Ireland, and was occupied by Tim Healy. Later, when Ireland became a Republic, the Lodge became known as Arus an Uachtaráin, the home of Ireland's Presidents, from Douglas Hyde as first President to Patrick Hillery, the sixth and present President of the Republic.

The Chief Secretary's Lodge is now the elegant residence of the American Ambassador.

Named 'Deerfield' now, it was in fact built in 1776. The Americans like the date, and are pleased with the idea that an Ambassador of a Republic which declared its independence in 1776, should have its Irish home in a house built in 1776.

They would approve, too, of the go-getting approach of John Blaquiere, the man who built it.

John Blaquiere arrived from England as Bailiff of Phoenix Park. He was given a four-roomed cottage in the Park, a potato patch, and enough land to graze a few cattle. In no time at all, Blaquiere added more acres. And built a wall round his property.

With £8,000 from the government, he built the house the Ambassador lives in.

All within two years of his arrival.

The only other official residence in the Park is the Papal Nunciature.

The American Ambassador and the Papal Nuncio were afforded the privilege in the early days of the State, because America and the Vatican were the first to recognise the newly declared Saorstat Eireann.

The Nunciature, the old Under-Secretary's Lodge, is in bad condition. The Papal Nuncio moved out to live in Cabra. There is talk, though, about putting the house right in an £8 million scheme planned for Phoenix Park.

The Main Road that runs almost dead straight from the Entrance Gate of Castleknock Gate is the work of Ormonde's successor, the Earl of Chesterfield, who became Viceroy in 1744.

He improved on Ormonde's handiwork, and in his days the Park became public property.

His intention is clearly – well nearly clearly – declared in the inscription on the Phoenix Monument he erected. The monument still stands, at the cross-roads between Arus an Uachtarain and the American Embassy. The inscription is in Latin – *Civium oblectamento campum rudem et incultum ornari iussit Philippus Stanhope, Comes de Chesterfield, Prorex.* Which, being translated says, "To delight the citizens, Philip Stanhope, Earl of Chesterfield, Viceroy, ordered this rough and uncultivated plain to be neatly set out."

Not that the citizens were unduly worried about the Latin or its translation. They were busy being delighted.

And they still are.

Brass bands in The Hollow. The Zoological Gardens that opened with a hyena, a wolf, a leopard and a pregnant lioness. And is now famous for breeding lions. And recently entertained two pandas, hoping the Dublin air might do them good. Polo, cricket, football, hurling on the 'Fifteen Acres', which in reality are two hundred acres. Motor-racing, horse-riding, walks along the Nature Trail, and making time to rest and enjoy the flowers in The People's Gardens. Feeding the ducks and swans on the lake in the Furry Glen, or picking blackberries from the Furry Glen right up to the Knockmaroon Gates. And the sight of the Dublin Mountains. From almost any place in the Park. Far out, the greens, greys, yellows, blacks and browns. The hedgerows, like thick threads, seaming them all together, patch to patch, like a cover on a too-tossed bed.

St. Mary's Hospital stands high on a hill near the Chapelizod Gates, and overlooks a calm, relaxing reach of the Liffey.

In days gone by, the building was the Hibernian Military School where boys trained for the British Army. The school is gone now, but the main building of the hospital and the square in front of it have lost none of their military character. The school chapel is still used, and the neat, militarily-tidy graveyard as carefully tended as in the days of old.

Down near Islandbridge Gate is Thomas Hill, where, once upon a time, there was a house known as The Phoenix, where the Viceroy lived in the days of Oliver Cromwell. Today it is the Magazine Fort.

At the opposite side of the Park, over at the North Circular Road entrance, what was once the

Constabulary Barracks is now the headquarters of the Garda Siochana.

Strictly speaking, religious services are banned in the Park. There have been two exceptions. The 'Fifteen Acres' was the site for Mass during the Eucharistic Congress in 1932. And, today, the giant cross set up for the occasion of Pope John Paul's visit to Ireland in 1979 marks the place where the Mass was celebrated.

There was no such holiness around the Vice-regal Lodge on May 6, 1822, the day of the Phoenix Park murders. Lord Frederick Cavendish was not long arrived as Chief Secretary in Ireland. Mr. Thomas Burke had been Under-Secretary for some years.

The two men strolled in the Park, near the Vice-regal Lodge.

In broad daylight they were stabbed to death by a group of men who came and went quickly, the speed and quietness of their fatal attack making it look no more than a drunken brawl.

The killers were members of a secret anti-English society called The Invincibles. They decided on knives rather than guns as weapons. The knives, two surgeon's knives, were specially imported from England for the killing.

The assassins might never have been discovered had not James Carey, one of their own members, turned informer. Carey gave the information that, some months after the assassination, led to the arrest and execution of his five companions.

It is said that Cavendish's widow sent a Rosary to each of the men before his execution.

There is a story that no executioner could be found to hang the men condemned for the murder. A notice was posted in Army 'orders', offering an immediate discharge and £1,000 to any soldier who would volunteer for the job. A sergeant volunteered. He completed the execution, got his discharge, and collected his £1,000. He was also given, and took, the wood that made the scaffold. He settled, it is said, in Chapelizod, and used the wood in building a house in which his family lived till it was demolished in a redevelopment scheme.

James FitzHarris, a cab-driver with the nickname 'Skin the Goat', who is reputed to have driven the group to and from the Park, was sentenced to sixteen years imprisonment as an accomplice.

Carey was pardoned for his part in the assassination. He was given a free passage to South Africa, but was himself eventually killed, on The Invincibles' direction, as his ship sailed into Durban.

The whole sad episode gave Dubliners a new word. 'Carey' is used to describe anybody who breaks faith and informs on his companions. A 'Carey' is a 'Judas'.

For long enough, a cross set in the road marked the assassination spot. It's gone now. And a jogger could pass the place, nowadays, unaware of his brush with history, thinking maybe of some refreshment when the exercise was ended.

Which thought conveniently brings the wandering mind back to the Brazen Head.

Some will say that the Brazen head is not just the oldest pub in Dublin, but the oldest in Europe. It was built in 1668, about fifty years before licensing laws were introduced in the city.

It looks its age, and there's a sadness about the place, in a clutter of posters and bric-a-brac.

A scribbled note on the door about "Poetry on sale at the bar – £1" is a reminder of the days when the likes of Brendan Behan and Patrick Kavanagh used to drink there.

Behind the bar hangs a bung-mallet, prominent in a conglomeration of lamps and brasses and bottles, hurley sticks, melodeons, a bodhran, and a notice declaring that only Irish music is allowed on the premises.

Nobody knows the origin of the three-foot figurine at the far end of the bar. It's been there as long as anybody remembers. Nowadays, the urn the figure of a lady leans against is a container for a cast-off bird's nest that in no way looks out of place.

Time chimes from the grandfather clock. But it's a begrudging kind of sound, as though the years had taken their toll. And each lifeless stroke follows reluctantly and uncertainly on the other till it has marked the hour, leaving behind the feeling that, for all the gaiety, conviviality and noise that must have filled its far-off days and nights, only the melancholy memories remain. The demolition orders that brought down Bridge Street have denuded the area sufficiently of houses and people to rob the Brazen Head of its clientele.

The bedrooms upstairs are empty now. No longer used. And there's no need anymore for the "Housemaid's Bell" kept polished in the narrow hall. It is no longer an inn.

There's every hope, though, that it will continue as a pub. In July 1986, it was bought by a Dublin businessman and his partner, with plans to refurbish the place.

So they'll still tell stories of the Brazen Head, and its associations with the enthusiasms, if not the successes, of Irish rebels... Of Napper Tandy who lived at Cornmarket at the top of the street, and how he plotted with Oliver Bond, whose house was, and still is, just across the road from the pub. Sorry tales of how the pair of them, with Lord Edward Fitzgerald and others, met in the Brazen Head to plot the rebellion of 1798. One of the members of the group, Thomas Reynolds, a rich landowner, was a spy. He informed on them. On March

12, 1798, Major Swan, on Reynolds' advice, swooped on Bond's house and arrested Oliver and fourteen others.

Lord Edward Fitzgerald managed to escape.

A reward of £1,000 was offered for information leading to his capture.

Francis Higgins, the 'Sham Squire' who lived on Stephen's Green, provided the information.

Lord Edward, he was able to tell, was a sick man, hidden in the house of Nicholas Murphy, a feather merchant in Thomas Street. (Today it is the offices of the Irish Agricultural Wholesale Society.)

Major Swan, Captain Ryan of the Bank of Ireland Yeomanry, and a soldier went into the bedroom to take their prisoner. Lord Edward drew a dagger. In the struggle, he wounded Ryan and Swan.

Major Sirr burst in with six soldiers, shot Lord Edward in the shoulder, overpowered him and took him prisoner.

Lord Edward died of his wounds in Newgate Jail on June 4, 1798. He was thirty-two years old, and left his lovely Lady Pamela a widow, staying at Moira House on Usher's Quay till she was deported shortly after her husband's burial in the vaults of St. Werburgh's church.

Moira House, the home of the Earl of Moira, was a grand house in its day. It is said to have been one of the most magnificently furnished houses in Ireland. In one room there was a window inlaid with mother-of-pearl.

Its grandeur continued until 1828, with Lord Edward and Lady Pamela Fitzgerald frequent visitors from their home at Frascati House, Blackrock.

Things changed when the house was taken over by the Association for the Prevention of Mendicity. They moved from their premises in Hawkins' Street, where for twelve years they had been providing free meals and cheap baths for the poor.

The Governors stripped the top floor off Moira House, took out the mother-of-pearl window, and called it The Mendicity Institute. And, for many a long year, the paupers of Dublin picked oakum for two meals a day. The Mendicity is gone now, and only the gates are left. All the grand houses are gone from Bridge Street, too. The place is almost deserted. Even number eleven is gone, the house where Jimmy O'Dea was born just one hundred years after the arrest of Oliver Bond a few doors down. Jimmy O'Dea was Dublin's king of comedy. An optician turned comedian who, in the guise of the widow Biddy Mulligan, gave Dublin a different way of looking at things.

It's a steep rise from the Liffey up to Cornmarket and High Street. But Bridge Street deliberately curves to take some of the hardship from the climb.

On the way up, there's Cook Street on the left-hand side,

running from Bridge Street to Winetavern Street.

Nowadays it's a wide-open thoroughfare, with the back of Oliver Bond flats and the Modern Schools on one side, and St. Audoen's church of the other.

Bare as it seems today, every inch of it echoes Dublin's history. Right back to the early days, when it was outside the city walls and got its name from being The Street of the Cooks.

A crowded, bustling, choking street, where the proprietors were known to supply the Prior of the Priory at St. Michael's Hill not only with lark pie, but with wine and ale from the taverns for which it was no less renowned.

In the late sixteen and seventeen hundreds, the street had a thriving trade in hasty marriages.

Tavern-keepers and shopkeepers fitted up chapels in their houses in which marriages might be performed. Some tavern-keepers retained the services of a clergyman, and sometimes they worked things with him on a profit-sharing basis.

Other clergy set up chapels in their own houses or lodgings. Others – "brandy-clergy" or "couple-beggars" as they were called – actually touted for business, and would marry any couple, drunk or sober, for half-a-crown, and ask no questions.

Like their renegade counterparts in England, the Fleet-parsons of London, these clergy caused havoc with the inheritance of great houses. The marriages, while irregular, were legal. And many a ne'er-do-well beguiled the daughter of a rich family into a marriage in Cook Street to gain her property.

Their activities eventually led to legislation that required couples to give due notice of their intention to marry. Marriage, from then on, could take place only in duly authorised premises, and only by licence or following the publication of Banns of Marriage. Solemnising a marriage under any other circumstance was considered a felony, punishable by transportation.

Cook Street had its chapels where Mass was said. It was noted for its Mass Houses, which existed because Roman Catholics were not allowed to say Mass publicly. The law relaxed a little when the floor of a house in the street collapsed while the priest was saying Mass. After that Roman Catholics were allowed to open proper chapels. In its time, the street has been the hub of Dublin's printing trade. Establishments like the "Sign of the Bible" and the "Sign of the Angel" turned out tracts to meet the religious needs of the 1700s.

In the next century printing gave way to coffin-making, when coffins came into general use.

At a time when Dublin was riddled with all kinds of sickness, and bereft of medical care, Cook Street led the way in 1721 by being the place where the Dublin

Charitable Infirmary began. It was later transferred to Jervis Street, where the hospital still stands. And still serves, making its own serious contribution to alleviate the modern terror of drug addiction.

Cook Street today, for the most part, is history recollected. On the south side of the street, though, history stands, waiting to be touched.

In the shape of St. Audoen's Arch. Here it is possible to stand in the only surviving gateway of the old city, and lean against part of the old city wall. The steps go up to St. Audoen's church, which has been hallowed ground since Celtic times, when St. Columcille's was built on the site before the Vikings came.

There is nothing left of St. Columcille's, but the 'lucky' stone in the porch of St. Audoen's is said to go back to Celtic times.

St. Audoen's itself was built in the twelfth century, and has had a good many ups and downs since then. At one time it had to be enlarged to cope with the increased population. Three hundred years later, it was so neglected the steeple almost fell down. There were days when the parish was crowded with the rich and well-heeled. Until the district changed, and their houses became the tenements where Dublin's poor were forced to live in grinding poverty, stinking dirt and dereliction.

As the parish church of The Liberties, it made more than a religious contribution to the life of its people. At 6 o'clock every morning, the bells of St. Audoen's – the oldest in Ireland – rang to get the people to work. They announced the time of the midday break at 11 o'clock. And at 8 pm they rang curfew.

In 1984 a major job of restoration was done on the church. The grounds are still being worked on.

In the church garden, on a sunny day, there's shelter from the wind. A dog barks, two youngsters play, watched by the baby cradled in his mother's arms. For all the grass is still wet from last night's rain, two lovers loll and talk and smile, and dream of life to come.

The new-laid cobble steps lead down from the garden, through a cobble-stone arch, to Bridge Street once again, where the hill turns up to Cornmarket.

Off to the right is Thomas Street, where Ailred founded Ireland's first hospital, and formed an order of Augustinian monks. John's Lane Church stands today where the hospital was, and Kelly's Timber Yard with its ornate arched entrance, on the opposite side of the street, was once the priory graveyard.

Thomas Street still has the feel of the old city about it. A market-place. Busy, crowded, narrow, noisy, gossipy. The dealers with their banter at the roadside stalls. Shoeshops, carpet shops, bric-a-brac, and people milling backwards and forwards.

Gordon and Thompson's shop is still there, recalling the days when Dublin girls thought themselves honoured to get a job in the shirt factory. And Frawleys, who long ago fitted, and still fit, the child out for First Communion and Confirmation.

St. Catherine's Church, a little further on, stands forlorn and grey, as though it were sad with too much history. Outside the church a stone pillar marks the spot where they built the scaffold to execute Robert Emmet on September 20, 1803.

Poor Emmet, who prepared so much to lead what turned out to be his half-hour rebellion. Seventy-four men he had, and just over £1,000. And plans to take Dublin Castle in a surprise attack.

They got nowhere near the Castle. The rebellion failed half-way down Thomas Street, when some of the rebels killed Lord Kilwarden as his carriage passed near St. Catherine's. They killed his nephew also. His daughter, though, who was travelling with the two men, escaped. She made her way to the Castle and raised the alarm.

Their leader, in his grey and white uniform and his cocked hat, was on the run.

Twenty-four years old and in love, he went to take leave of his fiancée Sarah Curran at her home in Rathfarnham. On August 25th he was arrested by Major Sirr at Harold's Cross, near what is now Emmet Bridge over the Grand Canal.

He was held for a month in Kilmainham Jail, until his trial before Lord Norbury in the Sessions House that still stands beside the Jail, and is still used as a Courthouse.

The charge against him was high treason. The trial lasted the best part of a day. It took the jury only a few minutes to reach its conclusion, and they felt no need to leave the courtroom. The verdict was 'Guilty'.

Emmet's counsel asked the Court to delay sentencing until the next day.

Lord Norbury refused. He pronounced sentence – that the prisoner be hanged and beheaded.

Had the prisoner anything to say why judgment of death and execution should not be awarded against him?

People talk about his reply as "Emmet's speech from the dock". But it was more than that. This was passion curbed and controlled to fit the measure of a word, emotion shaped to eloquence.

Six times Lord Norbury interrupted, and was still interrupting as the prisoner ended his speech. "Let no man write my epitaph... when my country takes her place among the nations of the earth, then, and not till then, let my epitaph be written..."

Robert Emmet was executed in public. There was nothing unusual about this. It was common practice at the time. It was also a practice to hang those involved in murder at or near the scene of the crime.

The front of St. Catherine's Church was chosen as the site for the scaffold, because it was nearest the spot where Lord Kilwarden and his nephew were killed. Robert Emmet, as leader of the rebellion, whether he liked it or not, was implicated with his men who had done the killing.

The chaplains, who had accompanied him in the carriage from the jail, now had their last words with him on the scaffold.

The executioner waited, gruesome, like a hunchback in a mask. The hunchback was caused by the protective basin round his shoulders for fear of being stoned by the crowd.

He kicked away the plank Robert Emmet stood on. Then he cut the dead body down, laid it on the scaffold, and decapitated it with a butcher's knife.

It was the sentence passed on Robert Emmet.

Gruesome indeed. And inhuman. But not unusual in the times. Murderers were hanged. Rebels were hanged and beheaded. Poisoners were hanged, drawn and quartered. And then the hangman held the severed head aloft, shouting from behind his mask, "Behold the head of a traitor". Women screamed. Men cursed. Dogs barked. And bedlam reigned in bloodstained Thomas Street.

They took the body back to Kilmainham Jail. To this day, nobody can be certain where Robert Emmet is buried. So far, no man has written his epitaph.

In 1966 the American Association of The Friends of Robert Emmet erected a bronze statue to his memory on Stephen's Green. The statue, simply inscribed "Robert Emmet", was placed opposite the house where he was born. The figure looks towards Grafton Street where, as a boy, he attended Mr. Samuel Whyte's School at No. 75, and later was a student at Trinity College at the end of Grafton Street.

The house itself was standing up to a few years ago, but, after long neglect, it collapsed.

Not far up from St. Catherine's, on the right-hand side, is No. 151, the site of an earlier success for Emmet's captor Major Sirr. It was here the Major arrested Lord Edward Fitzgerald. At Nicholas Murphy's home. Murphy, who was arrested at the same time, later died a pauper.

A few steps further on and there's Guinness'. On both sides of the road. All sixty-five acres of it.

To say what's made in Guinness' is stating the obvious. But it amounts to two million barrels a year. In terms of pints, that's staggering.

It could be said that it was holy water and the Church of Ireland that got Guinness started.

The Most Revd. Arthur Price, Archbishop of Cashel, bequeathed £100 to his godson Arthur Guinness, whose father was land agent to Dr. Price.

Twenty-seven-year-old Arthur set up a small brewery in Leixlip with the legacy.

Seven years later, in 1759, he bought Rainsford's brewery in St. James's Gate. It had been on the market, with no takers, for about ten years. Arthur Guinness took it on a nine thousand year lease at a rent of £45 a year. And, with a constant supply of water from St. James' Well in Kildare, he began the enterprise that is now the biggest brewery in the world, and which in the next year or two will be the most technologically advanced brewery in the world.

But Guinness, it ought to be said, are not just here for the beer.

In Dublin the Guinness family are famous and respected for their generosity to the city and its citizens. St. Stephen's Green, Iveagh House, St. Anne's Clontarf, are some of the gifts.

St. Patrick's Park, by the Cathedral, is the result of a slum clearance scheme by Guinness. The surrounding Iveagh Buildings are there because of an undertaking to provide the same number of dwelling units as had been demolished.

Today's Vocational School by St. Patrick's Park began in 1915 as the Iveagh Play Centre, and for years was known to children all over the city as The Bayno.

There has been a Guinness connection with St. Patrick's Cathedral for over two hundred years. It began with Arthur Guinness' gift of £250 to St. Patrick's Choir School. Benjamin Lee Guinness paid £150,000 for the restoration of the Cathedral.

Beyond Guinness' there's a fork in the road, by an ancient pillar. Once upon a time it was a sundial and drinking-fountain combined. The drinking-fountain has long since disappeared, the sundial is smothered by the trees that grow around it. But it is a focal-point for the tinkers when they have their horse fairs on an occasional summer's Sunday morning.

Off to the left is James' Street, and St. James' Hospital. Nowadays it's lively, airy, caring and healing.

But there is a lingering sadness in the Dubliner's memory of the place. "No. 1 James' Street", they called it, or "The Union", to take the harm out of what it really was – The Workhouse.

The high, grey, frightening, forbidding boundary wall is gone, and the place is open, bright and clean. Yet, somehow, the ghosts of days not all that long past still seem to haunt the place. Days when Dublin's poor slaved on a diet of gruel and bread-and-milk, and both staff and inmates were kept subservient with a cat-o'-nine-tails, and the threat of transportation or the madhouse.

Nor were the inmates always there of their own will and wish. A good many were rounded up in the nightly scouring of the city, and dragged, protesting, to endure the bitter charity of those who reckoned they were doing good.

The Foundling Hospital that was part of the Workhouse is gone, too, and the wheel where a broken, anonymous mother would put her illegitimate child, and then ring the bell to bring the porter to collect the child. And then she left, not knowing whether her infant would live or die, but fairly certain the child would be dead by the time it was twelve years old.

The turn to the right of the sundial leads down the hill to Bow Lane and St. Patrick's Hospital. Swift's Hospital it used to be called, and it was built with money the Dean bequeathed to found a hospital for lunatics.

Past the hospital and the Forty Steps – or Cromwell's Quarters as the alleyway of steps is officially known – Bow Lane becomes Kilmainham Lane.

And all along the left-hand side, the little houses seem to dangle at the edge of the road, constantly threatening to topple into the Camac River lazing its way through the valley below.

The lane runs up to Kilmainham. A place of stark contrasts. On one corner, the recently restored elegance of the Royal Hospital, Kilmainham Jail on the other.

The Jail stopped being used in the late 1920s. By 1960 it was a ruin. Until it was taken over by a committee who have organised its restoration with voluntary funds and labour.

It is now a museum, open to visitors on Sundays, and a shrine to the executed leaders of the 1916 Rising. There's a strange sadness in the place. An overwhelming sadness, made sadder by the guided tour that hurries, with potted, sorrow-laden history, from one prison memory to the next.

Parnell's room is there. And the chapel where Joseph Mary Plunkett married Grace Gifford on the morning of his execution. The peep-hole in the wall of the hangman's room, through which he 'measured' the condemned as they were marched along the corridor.

In the room where Robert Emmet awaited his trial, the story is told of poor Anne Devlin, his housekeeper at Butterfield House, Rathfarnham.

Not enough that she was half-hanged several times to reveal the whereabouts of Robert Emmet, she was taken to Kilmainham. And there, without trial, with no convictions, she was imprisoned for almost three years. She revealed nothing about Emmet or anybody else involved with him in the rebellion.

Even when it was obvious she would never give any information, she was still kept in the jail, the story goes, by Dr. Travers, as a punishment for spurning his advances. Eamonn de Valera was the last prisoner in the jail. He was, in fact, a prisoner there twice. First in 1916, imprisoned by the British. And then during the Civil War a few years later.

There is an understandable resentment on the part of the Jail Committee that no public money has been spent on its restoration, whereas the Royal Hospital on the far side of road has had £21 million spent on restoring it.

When Charles II built the Royal Hospital in 1684, it cost £26,000 He built it where the Hospitaller Knights once had their Priory.

It was established as a home for veteran soldiers. And so it continued for almost two-hundred-and-fifty years. The last of the veterans was moved to the Royal Hospital, Chelsea, shortly after the formation of the Irish Free State.

And the building was neglected. Until now, fifty years later, it is restored and open to the public for the first time in its history. In times gone by, outsiders of no less importance than Dean Swift had to face the challenge of an armed sentry. Now they're welcome, so long as they pay the entry fee.

The Royal Hospital is grandeur. Inside and out. The long drive, the terrace, and the sense of space. Inside, the Great Hall, the Chapel. And the memorial to Lord Robert's horse that was decorated three times in the course of its military career with the Field Marshal.

There is a temptation to dally and enjoy it all. It's been a long journey out from the Cornmarket, so there might be an excuse to stand and stare.

But it is time to go back to Cornmarket, and take the route to the left.

But maybe not directly back. For on the way there's Meath Street and Francis Street.

Meath Street has hardly changed. Even the Liberty's Creche building that the Quakers started in 1893 is still there. Bustling Meath Street, its crowded shops and bazaars, its busy dealers by the roadside.

But Francis Street is almost unrecognisable. The Tivoli Cinema is closed and bricked-up. The 'Tivvo' as they called it, where before the days of television they ran a serial film – the folly-er upper – with a cliff-hanger ending that brought you back to queue in the rain with the shouting kids for next week's episode.

The whole street has changed, the traffic races through where once it was difficult enough to walk for thronging people.

Even Mr. Mushatt's is gone. Mushatt's, where you could buy a tablet, a pill, a powder or a bottle that would cure anything from chilblains to consumptive coughs, from nits in the hair to callouses and bunions and blotchy skin. It's antiques now in Francis Street. Bits and pieces of old Dublin, dug up done up and turned into business. Big business, in some cases, for Francis Street can now boast an antiques emporium, a supermarket where a chaise longue plays companion to a Georgian fire-surround, and a Jacob's Biscuits display case has no less honour than the inlaid escritoire.

The Iveagh Market, though, is still there, with its imposing front looking a bit the worse for wear, but as busy as ever.

In one part, small and quite separated, it's meat and fish and eggs. The rest is clothes, shoes, pictures, books, bric-a-brac, radios, televisions, ties, table-lamps and furniture. All second-hand. Even the furniture. Though, as she says herself, "If it makes y'feel better, it's antique".

It has all the appearance of a jumbo-sized jumble sale. As though all the cast-offs of Dublin had been gathered under one roof.

Stacked high here and there on the floor. Piled on tables. Hanging like stalactites from the corner posts and cross-bars of the stalls. And draped, but always within convenient reach, all over the walls. And up there with the coats and suits and gaberdenes, a wedding dress, forlorn and lonely with an out-of-place look that would play havoc with a romantic heart.

It's business everywhere. Except, maybe, at the furniture and the book stall.

The books themselves run the gamut from theology to titillation, but there's no real demand.

Not that there's much being sold at the stall next door. What matters is the chat from one side of the stall to the other. Small, wizened and full of experience she was. And the stall-holder was glad she'd come in. And she oohed and aahed and aw-god-help-hered through the saga of the rash on the stall-holder's youngest one's face.

And wisdom waited, biding her time till the tale was told. And then she spoke, like an oracle. "I'd leave off badin' it, if I was you."

"D'y think so...?"

"Sure the wather's ony spreadin' it, whatever it is... and specially hot wather..."

"You could be right there."

"No. What you want is calomine lotion. Plenty o' calomine lotion. Me mother, God rest her, was a great believer in calomine lotion. And so am I..."

"I'll try that then."

"You can take my word. Put plenty o' calomine on, and she'll be right be Tuesda."

At the other end of the stall she was selling lingerie. White, silk lingerie.

"Hardly worn," says she, holding each intimate piece aloft to be approved of by customer and onlookers alike.

"At three pounds, you're gettin it for nothin'..."

The customer wasn't sure.

"I'm tellin ye..."

The customer still wasn't sure.

"Two-fifty, then... and I'll put them in a box..."

The onlookers thought it was a bargain.

"With them on, he won't know ye..." offered one of them.

"And at two-fifty," explained the customer," he won't want to know..."

"But he'll go mad about the box..." assured another. And they all guffawed. And she paid her two-fifty.

Outside the back gate of the market, it's hard to decide which way to go first, for all kinds of places beckon all at once.

Not least the area behind the market itself. The neat streets of terraced houses, tidy and bright, tucked so quietly away from the busy thoroughfare you'd hardly notice they were there. And here and there, a hidden gem like Power Square.

Down the hill, over the roofs of the houses, the majesty of St. Patrick's Cathedral, its clock plainly visible, telling the time in blue and gold. St. Patrick's, only a loud shout away, need not be surprising, of course. It is to be expected, with the Market Gate on the corner of Dean Swift Square.

A ninety-degree turn... a right-angled turn to the left, as the Dublin man explains... and there's another cathedral. Christ Church Cathedral, and its covered bridge arching across St. Michael's Hill to the old Synod Hall.

There was a time when it was impossible to see Christ Church from here. But that's a long time ago, when Back Lane and High Street in between meant shops, workshops, houses, alleyways and thronging people.

Only the medieval twist remains to tell how old Back Lane is. And Tailors Hall. Nearly three hundred years old, Tailors Hall was built by the Guild of Tailors. It has been used for all kinds of things since.

It was the meeting place of the Back Lane Parliament that was formed by the alliance of the Catholic Committee with Wolfe Tone and the United Irishmen.

It has been a Freemasons' Lodge and a Dancing Academy in its time, and up to about twenty years ago, the rafters of the main hall rang, on Friday nights and Sunday afternoons and evenings, with the lusty singing of Moody and Sankey hymns when it was used as a Gospel Hall. Aer Lingus used it as a restaurant for a while. Now it is the headquarters of An Taisce, so the fond hope is that it will be carefully preserved, along with its entrance gate and arch.

Lamb Alley runs from the back gate of the Market to join Cornmarket where part of the old city wall juts out like a piece of history that refuses to go away. The wall, in its day, was not only part of the city boundary, but was also the outer wall of the original Newgate Jail.

Across the road from here is Bridge Street, the spot we've been coming back to since we left Kilmainham and the Royal Hospital.

But stay on this side of the road. St. Audoen's, from here, is partly hidden by the slope of the hill. And beyond, away among the slates and bricks and shadows that shape the city skyline, the bright green of the Four Courts' copper dome.

Sixty-four feet in diameter, the dome took a battering when the Free State Army bombarded the Four Courts in the Civil War of 1922. The interior was gutted, the Records Office destroyed, when, they say, the documents and papers of Ireland's past were blown sky-high by bombs, tattered, burnt and lost for ever. It took ten years to restore the Four Courts.

Beside St. Audoen's, dwarfing what can be seen of the little church, is St. Audoen's.

That's not a misprint. Nor even eye trouble. It's fact. The first St. Audoen's is old and Church of Ireland. The second newer, and Roman Catholic.

It's a kind of double-take, for whatever reason, that characterises the area. There are two St. James' in James' Street. Old St. Catherine's is in Thomas Street. There's another in Meath Street. The tower of old St. Nicholas' stands opposite Christ Church. The newer church is in Francis Street.

Although it would be difficult to swing a censer in the gap between one St. Audoen's and the other, the old one is in Cornmarket, the newer one in High Street.

There's not a lot left on that side of High Street. There's nothing at all on this. Tailors Hall is all that stands in the space from here to Christ Church Place.

Everything that could be demolished has been demolished to make room for the motor-car. And what was once the High Street of the city, in every sense of the word, is now no more than a traffic-way.

Way back in the second century, it was part of the boundary that divided Ireland North and South, between Ulster's King Conn of the Hundred Battles, and Mogh, King of Leinster.

The Vikings developed the place till it became something of an industrial estate. Merchants and manufacturers lived and worked there.

Later generations built the Market Cross where High Street joined the junction of Nicholas Street, Winetavern Street and Skinner's Row, as Christ Church Place was known. It was part of the route that led from Bridge Street and Newgate, through Skinner's Row to Dublin Castle. They held Wolfe Tone's wake in No. 56 High Street. The party went on for two nights, till the authorities reckoned it had lasted long enough, and ordered that Wolfe Tone be buried immediately, and as privately as possible. Wolfe Tone would have enjoyed that. It was certainly different from anything the authorities had planned for him in the way of death.

Captured in the French invasion fleet that arrived in Bantry Bay to support the United Irishmen's rising in 1798, he was sentenced to be hanged.

The idea of dying did not frighten him. Indeed, years earlier, he reckoned he would eventually be hanged. And disembowelled. But now, his soldierly instincts and pride resented the disgrace of hanging. He asked, instead, that as a French officer, he should be shot.

The request was refused. He avoided the ignominy by cutting his throat with a penknife on the execution morning.

Matilda, the clergyman's daughter to whom he was happily married, was left a widow to look after her children now bereft of their father.

The junction at the end of High Street is as busy as ever it was. Now, though, it's traffic that snarls for right of way. In days gone by, it was traders at the Market Cross. Or criers publishing papal bulls and government decrees. Or even reading wills. And sometimes a dejected figure in a white shift, doing public penance. The public stocks were there. They're now in the crypt of Christ Church Cathedral. They were last used in 1864 and, rumour has it, the victim then was a little girl, being punished for stealing an apple.

When Christ Church Place was known as Skinner's Row, the Tholsel stood on the corner. It was pulled down in 1806, but for the five hundred years it existed, it served as toll-house, town hall and jail. It also had its own gallows. And was a favourite starting-point for whipping law-breakers, with the condemned tied to the tail-end of a cart that dragged him down Dame Street to the Parliament House in one direction, or the length of Thomas Street in the other.

It was a dilapidation by the time it was demolished. The statues of Charles II and James II, however, withstood the ravages of time and neglect. When the Tholsel was gone, they were moved across the road to Christ Church Cathedral. They're now in the crypt, where James' statue keeps company with the Tabernacle used at the Mass celebrated at the monarch's direction during his ambitious, but unexpectedly short, sojourn in Dublin.

The crypt itself is said to be the remnant of the old Holy Trinity Church King Sitric encouraged Bishop Donatus to build in 1037.

Whether or aye, it is an integral part of the cathedral and its history.

It has the same preserving properties as St. Michan's

vaults on the far side of the Liffey, though it has not the same dramatic evidence.

Christ Church crypt, however, is a place where people meet and eat and drink. At the "Cat and Rat", named after the cat and rat found some long time ago behind the organ, and preserved, leather-like, in the vaults, near enough not to go unnoticed by the drinkers.

Nowadays, the drink is coffee, tea or Coca Cola.

There were days when it was very different, and the crypt had all the appearance of being an annexe to any one of Winetavern Street's one-hundred-and-thirty-seven taverns, while upstairs, in the cathedral, the merchants did their business deals.

It all sounds unthinkable, nowadays. But, for all the complaints about it, then, it was not at all out of the way. They did the same in England. In places like York Minster and Durham Cathedral.

The nave of St. Paul's Cathedral, London, was practically a public thoroughfare. The chapels and cloisters were clogged with merchandise, and some were used as workshops. Lawyers had their own pillars, and met their clients there. Out-of-work servants used "St. Paul's Walk" as the best place for finding a new employer. Not to mention the brawling that went on even during the time of divine service, and the cattle and horses that were driven through the church.

Penny fines were tried as a way of stopping the abuse. But they did not work. Even Acts of Parliament failed. The great Fire of London in 1666 was the only thing that put an end to the scandal. The fire destroyed St. Paul's and "St. Paul's Walk" with it.

Christ Church crypt, by comparison, was "Happy Hour" stuff.

The cathedral was begun by Strongbow in 1172, and took fifty years to complete. Its proper title is The Cathedral of the Holy Trinity, commonly called Christ Church.

A few years after building began, Strongbow died. Archbishop Laurence O'Toole, his patron in the enterprise, conducted the burial service.

There are memorials to both men in the cathedral.

Strongbow's is strange, indeed, for beside the full-size figure of a knight, there lies the upper-half of another body, the hands pressed against the stomach.

The knight is reckoned to be Strongbow. There is an argument about the half-size figure. Some say it represents Strongbow's wife. Some say it's Strongbow's son, and tell a story to explain how the lad is only half there.

Son of Strongbow the warrior who feared nobody, the boy asked and was given charge of a cavalry troop preparing for battle. When battle commenced,

however, the inexperienced young soldier took fright, and turned to run away.

Strongbow saw it, reckoned the disgrace his son would bring on the family. And prevented it by cutting his son down with his sword.

The story goes on to say that Strongbow later repented, and ordered the monument as a constant memorial to his sense of guilt and sorrow for his awful deed.

One explanantion is as good as another. But there are those who accept neither. And they will say that the half-size figure is no more than a container for Strongbow's intestines.

An iron casket in the St. Laud Chapel at the East end of the cathedral is said to contain Archbishop Laurence O'Toole's heart, put there by his followers who seem to have taken his dying wish rather too literally. The Archbishop, it appears, was travelling home from a visit to Rome. He arrived at Eu in Normandy. There he took sick and died. Almost his last words to his followers were that his heart be buried back in his beloved cathedral. It is the only holy relic left in Christ Church. There might have been others had Archbishop George Browne not responded so eagerly to the orders of Henry VIII.

George Browne's task was to destroy the holy relics in both Dublin cathedrals.

And included in the things that fed his bonfire was the Bachall Iosa, the staff of Jesus. Sometimes known as St. Patrick's Crozier, it was a staff purported to have been covered with gold and jewels by Jesus himself, who gave it to a hermit to be eventually delivered to St. Patrick. It found its way to Christ Church via the Normans and Armagh.

The same bonfire destroyed the gold circlet that was used in the cathedral fifty years earlier to crown Lambert Simnel King of England.

Crowned in Dublin as Edward VI, the new king might have been wiser to have reigned in Dublin. A month after his coronation, he returned to England, where he was arrested as a pretender, and spent the remainder of his days turning the spits in the kitchens of Henry VIII.

Christ Church began as a priory, with its monks and an abbott. The abbott lived on St. Michael's Hill where the Synod Hall is now. And he lived well, his table kept stocked by the cooks of Cook Street, the ale-brewers of Winetavern Street, and the wine importers of Rochelle Street, as Back Lane was known.

It escaped the heavy hand of Henry VIII during his dissolution of the monasteries. It changed its status, and became a cathedral with a dean and chapter.

A king was crowned there. Kings worshipped there. For long enough Parliament enacted its laws there. The high and mighty came and went. And the poor were not forgotten. And poor enough there were in the city. All ages. All stages of poverty.

Some say that Kirk's marble sculpture at the west end of the church sentimentalises poverty. Maybe it does. It is still a fine work, though. A lad standing by an urn. A beggar lad, apprehensive, skimpy in his rags, a tear just about to fall from his urchin's eye.

It is a memorial to the philanthropist Thomas Abbott. It also places Dublin's beggars solidly in Dublin's history. For they are there. Since time immemorial, and, by the looks of things, in perpetuity.

Beggars Bush, on the edge of Ringsend, gets its name from the days when Dublin's beggars congregated there. Some genuine and honest, others crooked and capable of all kinds of skulduggery, including pickpocketing and mugging. There were times when Dublin's beggars could obtain a licence to beg in certain areas of the city. And there were other times when they were transported as slaves to the West Indies.

The Vagrancy Act, drawn up to cope with the vast numbers of beggars that crowded into the city during the Famine, is still sometimes invoked by the Gardai. But the buskers in Grafton Street and Henry Street will tell you it's mainly against them.

Maybe things were different in Abbott's day, and every beggar in Dublin was genuinely in need.

Nowadays it's hard to tell. And in a city that's almost instinctively generous to anybody in need, there's a feeling that an awful lot of people are being conned.

Seven hundred years of history in a city of changing fortunes, and suffering wear and tear which, when it wasn't totally ignored, was slovenly attended to, meant that by the 1800s Christ Church was in a bad way. The fabric was in a sad state, and Dublin's slums had encroached to within a few feet of its walls.

If a porter brewer was to restore St. Patrick's, it was a whiskey distiller who was the salvation of Christ Church. Sir Henry Roe undertook the cost of the massive task. The cathedral was closed for seven years while the work was done. The final bill of £200,000 ran wildly beyond the original estimate, and nearly bankrupted Henry Roe. But the place looked good. The slums around were cleared, the grounds opened up, revealing the ruins of the old Chapter House.

The Chapter House ruins are still there, enclosing stones from the old building, each one carefully numbered by the excavator. But totally useless for all that. The excavator's plan is lost.

About the time of Roe's restoration, the Synod Hall was built at the top of St. Michael's Hill. It incorporated the tower of St. Michael's, and was joined to the cathedral by the covered bridge that spans St. Michael's Hill and forms an archway into Winetavern Street.

The Synod Hall was the place where the Church of Ireland conducted its legislative business. Until recently, when it was given over to an enterprising group to be developed as a museum, an arts centre and a venue for Medieval banquets.

Today, eight hundred years after it was built, and nearly a thousand years after the first church appeared on the site, Christ Church stands, bright, clean and majestic. It has been refurbished. This time the cost was met by public subscription. From all sides of the denominational barriers.

On either end of the cathedral are Winetavern Street and Fishamble Street, but both are really only barbs that snag the memory, now.

Winetavern Street is a living lie. For, today, there is neither wine nor tavern in the place that once boasted almost one-hundred-and-fifty drinking houses. And all that is left to recall the heady days is Adam and Eve's Church that backs into the street from Merchant's Quay.

The church, in fact, is dedicated to the Immaculate Conception. Its nickname goes back to the days when Roman Catholics were forbidden to attend Mass in public, and instead attended Mass houses set up in taverns. Adam and Eve's was one of those taverns.

The street is completely empty now. Everything's gone. Even the Irish House from the Wood Quay corner.

A childhood in Dublin was excited by the round towers strung along the top of O'Meara's Irish House, and learnt history incidentally from the stucco-work panels on the facade. Like Grattan addressing the Irish Parliament, or Daniel O'Connell, and Erin weeping on a stringless harp.

They're gone now, and kept in the Guinness Museum. The public house is gone too. Demolished, like everything else of Wood Quay, to make room for the new Civic Offices.

The Wood Quay development in the 1960s caused a terrible row in Dublin. For some it was the desecration of the sacred site where Dublin began.

Fishamble Street, at the east end of the cathedral, was a kind of residential area for the Vikings, their wooden houses set in long, narrow gardens reaching down to the Liffey. The models in the National Museum give some idea of what they looked like.

Kennan's Foundry is about the only thing left in Fishamble Street. And it's hard to believe it was once a thriving, thronging place. And with a smell all its own when they sold fish there, and Dublin beggars slept under the fish stalls.

One of the oldest streets in the city, it has written itself into Dublin's history.

Swift's "Drapier's Letters" were published in an alley off the street. Henry Grattan was born there in 1746, the year after Swift died.

James Clarence Mangan was born there. A sad man.

With the face of a corpse that was not improved by his bleached hair. He was an opium addict and spent a good deal of his time drinking in The Bleeding Horse in Camden Street. A sad poet, too, still remembered as the writer of "Dark Rosaleen".

He died in the cholera epidemic that followed the Famine of 1847. He is amongst the poets honoured by memorials in St. Stephen's Green.

Fishamble Street and Handel's "Messiah" go together. It was first performed there. On April 13, 1742. In the Music Hall which William Neal had opened only the previous October.

Handel had been invited to Dublin for six concerts organised to raise money for charity, and the story is that he wrote the "Messiah" especially for his Dublin visit.

The concert was a sell-out. Seven hundred people were packed into a hall barely able to take six hundred. To make the extra space, the ladies were asked not to wear their hoops.

Dublin rose to the occasion, and thrilled to the performance by the combined choirs of St. Patrick's and Christ Church Cathedrals, unaware that what they heard was Handel's fulfilment of a boyhood dream to set the whole story of Jesus to music.

Old, sick, poor, and considered to be finished as a composer was Handel when he felt the urge to write the Messiah. For twenty-four days he wrote. Hardly eating, hardly sleeping. Until the day he called his servant, and, with tears rolling down his face, exclaimed "It is finished. I saw the gates of heaven open, and I heard the angels sing the Hallelujah Chorus."

In 1884 the top part of Fishamble Street was demolished to join Christ Church Place to Dame Street. The result was Lord Edward Street, joining Cork Hill and leading into Dame Street.

Cork Hill means City Hall. Which is a pity, because the roadway is not broad enough to allow it to be seen and enjoyed properly. Look at it from Capel Street, across the bridge, with Parliament Street as a kind of viewing tunnel.

As its name suggests, City Hall is the meeting place of the City's Corporation. Their being there, though, is the result of a happy coincidence.

The building was erected, in the first place, to accommodate the merchants when the business of the city was concentrated at the west end. It was the Royal Exchange.

As Dublin developed, however, the business moved eastward into the new heart of the city. The merchants moved with it, and left the Exchange deserted.

The Corporation, up to now, had met in the Tholsel. But by 1806, the Tholsel was in a ruinous state. The Corporation moved. They demolished the Tholsel and

established themselves in the Royal Exchange, which has been City Hall ever since.

Today, the Stock Exchange is in Anglesea Street, off Dame Street. In banking country, as it were, with the recently erected Central Bank building nearby in Dame Street, and the headquarters of the Bank of Ireland not much further down in College Green.

The Bank of Ireland building is the old Parliament House. Four architects were involved in building it.

The Architect General for Ireland, Thomas Burgh, was asked to draw up plans to replace delapidated Chichester House where the Irish Parliament met.

Sir Arthur Chichester, Viceroy of Ireland, had bought the house from Sir George Carew. Carew had built it as a hospital for old soldiers who had fought in the campaigns of Elizabeth I against the O'Neills and O'Donnells. It was never used as a hospital. Instead, Carew lived in it himself, until he sold it to Chichester.

When Chichester asked Burgh to plan a new building, Burgh considered himself too old to get involved in so big a task. He passed it over to twenty-eight-year-old Edward Lovett Pearce, who began planning in 1727.

Work began in 1729, but Pearce died a few years later. The building was completed by 1735, under the supervision of its third architect, Arthur Dobbs.

The fourth architect was James Gandon who, some years later, built the extension on the Westmoreland Street side to accommodate the House of Lords.

It is part of the quirkiness of history that, in this very building, Grattan's Parliament voted to set up a state bank. This bank, the Bank of Ireland, was established in St. Mary's Abbey, with a capital of a million-and-a-half pounds.

When the Parliament was brought to an end, following the Act of Union in 1800, the building was no longer needed.

The Bank of Ireland promptly bought it for forty-thousand pounds.

But we've rushed down Dame Street and not noticed one of Dublin's institutions, the Olympia Theatre, which to this day continues the traditions begun by Dan Lowry back in the 1890s.

Dan Lowry opened his Star of Erin music hall in Crampton Court. It closed in 1897, but soon opened again as the Empire Palace Theatre, with its entrance now in Dame Street. The theatre is still the same. Now it is the Olympia. And it still stands almost opposite the City Hall.

Dublin Castle is behind the City Hall.

The fortress the Vikings built on the high ground commanding the Black Pool, the Ford of the Hurdles and the land about is long, long gone.

Henry de Loundres began replacing it shortly after Christ Church Cathedral was built, and generations after him made their individual contribution, demolishing, rebuilding, or adding as they saw the need.

What stands today is the result of patching and mending, repairs, additions, adaptations and replacements.

It's easy, walking in the Upper and Lower Yard, to imagine the grandeur that paraded there in a bygone day. But there's a jaded air about the place, a melancholy, maybe, that clings to the bits and pieces of faded aristocracy.

No matter how you look at it, the Castle is invader's property. Yet, in its own way, it is a standing memorial to generations who never quite took their invaders seriously, and who can, when it suits them, gild history with a touch that makes it seem no more than incidental.

The State Apartments are magnificent, restored and cared-for as they are. And if yesterday's people came back today, they would not feel out of place in their surroundings. The throne room is still there, and the throne, two hundred years old. The portraits of the viceroys adorn the walls as they always did. The lovely Lady Castlemaine has a place to herself, still mistress in her own room.

They might be surprised, though, by St. Patrick's Hall. The banners of the Knights of St. Patrick still grace its walls. The three ceiling paintings are there: St. Patrick preaching; the coronation of George III; the Irish Chieftains paying homage in the time of Henry II. But now the Hall is geared to cope with the technological age and its demands, if not for instant understanding, at least for instant communications. Now Heads of State can meet there, and have simultaneous translations of what's being said. And the world outside, if need be, can have instant sound and vision.

Banquets they have there which visitors from the Castle's past would understand. But to witness, in St. Patrick's Hall, the swearing-in of the President of the Irish Republic...! As yer wan back in the Iveagh Market might say, "If they were alive today, they'd turn in their graves".

Dublin Castle is in the parish of St. Werburgh, and in the days before the Castle had a Chapel of its own, the Lord Lieutenant had his own stall in the parish church.

The church gives its name to the street it stands in, and one way or another has shared in Dublin's history almost since Dublin began.

It shared the parish's excitement in 1706 when fire appliances were introduced in the city. There are two of the appliances, no bigger than a handcart, in the church porch.

Lord Edward Fitzgerald is buried in its vaults. And by history's strange irony, Major Sirr, who brought about his downfall, is buried in the churchyard.

Hosea Guinness, the eldest of Arthur Guinness' sons, did not follow his father into the brewing business at St. James's Gate. Instead, he was ordained in the Church of Ireland, and served a curacy in St. Werburgh's.

Hoey Court, in the parish, was the birthplace of Jonathan Swift.

Nobody in the parish in 1667 could have guessed that the newborn infant would grow up to be Dean of the Cathedral a couple of hundred yards from his own doorstep.

St. Patrick's itself was almost five hundred years old by the time Jonathan Swift was born.

There had been a church on the site from the days of St. Patrick himself. Built on a strip of land between two branches of the River Poddle, it was soon called St. Patrick's on the Island.

It was also outside the city walls. A fact Archbishop John Comyn noticed when he decided it was time to escape the authority the Viceroy and Parliament had over Christ Church Cathedral.

He made his move in 1191. He declared St. Patrick's a collegiate church, and put up a new stone building. Nearly twenty years later his successor, Henry de Loundres, raised St. Patrick's to the status of a cathedral.

It was not popular. Two cathedrals in a city is bad enough. Two cathedrals within half a mile of each other is asking for trouble. The trouble was not lessened when the newly-built Palace of St. Sepulchre, beside the cathedral, became the Archbishop's residence.

The hassle went on for about eighty years. Till 1300, when it was arranged that Christ Church would be the Cathedral of the See of Dublin, with the right to consecrate the Archbishop of Dublin, and St. Patrick's would be the National Cathedral.

And so it is today. Except for the Palace of St. Sepulchre. Not that there is much of it left, but the little there is – the entrance gate and boundary wall – has been incorporated in Kevin Street Garda Station.

Always a bit on the independent side, St. Patrick's did not take easily to the attempts of Henry VIII at Reformation in the Church. And for years St. Patrick's paid the consequences. Henry confiscated its revenues. Edward VI reduced it to the level of a parish church. At one stage, Sir John Perrott wanted to do away with it altogether, and use the building as a university. Perrott was said to be an illegitimate son of Henry VIII. At any rate, that's what they called him in Dublin. Cromwell's cavalry stabled their horses in the cathedral. Fifty years later William III arrived to give thanks for his victory at the Boyne. The red-upholstered chair he sat on for the service is still in the Lady Chapel.

Enter Jonathan Swift. Patriot, pamphleteer, satirist, wit,

author of "Gulliver's Travels." The man who started what must have been the first "Buy Irish" campaign, when he encouraged Irish clergy to buy only Irish cloth for their robes, and coined the phrase, "burn everything English but their coal."

All this he did during his thirty-two years as Dean of St. Patrick's. All this is remembered.

What is often forgotten, though, is that he was a devout, disciplined, compassionate pastor to his people who, in their turn, loved and respected him.

Maybe he was not best pleased with Dublin as a city. But in his day, Dublin was not a city with which to be pleased. It served the bulk of its citizens badly.

It's easy, at this distance, to be coy and sentimental about the Coombe and the Liberties in the old days. They were bad days. The Liberties experienced the painful meaning of industrial recession and market depression before even the terms were invented. It was not just poverty. It was destitution. And the wonder is that anybody survived at all. That some did is due in a measure to Jonathan Swift and others like him.

The Dean of St. Patrick's gave the poor the best part of his income, including the royalties from all his writings except "Gulliver's Travels". He knew the slums of Dublin intimately, for they now encircled his cathedral. He walked their streets, having deliberately filled his pockets with coins to distribute to the poor he met. He used his own money to set up a fund to help small businessmen with interest-free loans that were repaid at a shilling a week. And bequeathed most of his estate – £11,000 – to build St. Patrick's Hospital.

He died on October 19, 1745. For two days mourning Dublin filed past his lying-in-state, for all he asked to be buried as quietly and as privately as possible.

He was buried at midnight. In St. Patrick's.

He wrote his own epitaph. A note beside his memorial in the cathedral supplies both Swift's own Latin composition and an English translation. What was said at his funeral, though, reflects the real man. "He lived a blessing. He died a benefactor. And his name will ever live an honour in Ireland."

One hundred and twenty years after Jonathan Swift died, the cathedral was on the verge of collapse.

It was saved by Benjamin Lee Guinness, who not only paid the £150,000 bill, but himself planned a good deal of the restoration.

It was when the Guinness family started the slum-clearance scheme round the cathedral in 1910 that they found the slab marking the site of St. Patrick's well.

The story of the well is that St. Patrick and some companions were returning from Wicklow to Armagh. They stopped to rest at this spot. The companions complained to Patrick that the water from the marsh was not fit to drink. As much in need of a drink himself, the saint caused a fountain of fresh water to spring forth.

The slab is in the cathedral now, by the steeple, as near to its original site as possible.

A solid reminder of the past. Like the door with the hole in it that greets you as soon as you enter the church.

It goes back to the days of the feuds between the Fitzgeralds, Earls of Kildare, and the Butlers, Earls of Ormonde.

Fitzgerald had been trying to bring the bitter squabbling to an end. He invited Butler to St. Patrick's for peace talks. Butler came. But while the two leaders were talking, Butler's men attacked Fitzgerald's men. The fight spread into the cathedral. Butler suspected treachery, and took refuge in the Chapter House.

Fitzgerald tried to reason with the man through the thick door. Butler did not respond. Fitzgerald then broke a hole in the door with an axe so that they could both shake hands as a mark of good faith. Butler would not respond, still convinced it was all a trick. Till Fitzgerald stuck his own arm through the hole.

The action added a new saying to the Dubliner's already colourful speech. "Chancing your arm," means having a go, taking a shot in the dark.

Across the Close from the cathedral is the Choir School. Founded in 1432 by Archbishop Talbot, it recently lost a playground to make way for an extension to accommodate its increasing number of students.

Further along the Close, wedged between the end of St. Patrick's graveyard and Kevin Street Garda Station, is Marsh's Library.

Strictly speaking, it is the Library of St. Sepulchre. It gets its unofficial name in memory of Narcissus Marsh who founded it in 1701, not long after he had resigned as Provost of Trinity College, and had become Archbishop of Dublin.

Marsh's is the oldest library in Ireland. Its layout has hardly changed over the years. The cubicles in which visitors were locked as they read are still there, as well as some of the chains that kept the books securely in the library.

It has something like twenty-five thousand books, and many manuscripts, most of which go back to the fifteenth and sixteenth centuries, and afford magnificent examples of book binding. Swift's death mask is there, and the table he is said to have used when he wrote "Gulliver's Travels".

It also has a ghost. Or maybe that was a tale told to local schoolboys to keep them from annoying the librarian by too-frequent visiting.

The ghost, they say, is the ghost of Narcissus Marsh himself, still searching the shelves to find the book in which his niece put her farewell note as she was leaving her uncle and the Palace of St. Sepulchre.

Grace Marsh was nineteen, and her uncle's housekeeper. Until the night of September 10, 1695, between eight and nine o'clock, when she sneaked out of the Palace and married Chas. Proby, vicar of Castleknock, in a tavern.

Despite the inauspicious start, however, she seems to have lived happily ever after. And lived to be eighty-five.

From the Library, through Kevin Street, Upper and Lower, and Cuffe Street, to St. Stephen's Green, is a comfortable ten or fifteen minute walk. But only with a discipline that resists all distractions on the way.

The Meath Hospital, for instance, built on the Dean's Cabbage Patch, or "Naboth's Vineyard", as Jonathan Swift used to call it. And opposite the hospital, Camden Row, with old St. Kevin's Churchyard, its sad recollections of the Penal Days, and its reminders of the saint from lovely Glendalough.

Wait too long to cross to Cuffe Street, and Whitefriar Street chapel beckons. Father Spratt's church, which he built in 1827 on the site of a thirteenth century Carmelite church.

A Dublin man himself, baptised in St. Catherine's, Meath Street, it was Fr. Spratt who found the statue of Our Lady of Dublin.

The statue began its history in St. Mary's Abbey. It disappeared when the Abbey suffered in the dissolution of the monasteries. It was not seen again till 1824, when Fr. Spratt discovered it in a junk shop, bought it, and two years later put it in Whitefriar Street church.

For a while it looked as though all that would be left of Cuffe Street would be the name. Only two buildings remained. Gorman's pawnshop and the Bricklayers' Hall.

Gorman's – or Meredith's as it was called before it changed hands – for generations was part of the economic system of thousands of Dublin families.

Then Gorman's was demolished. The Bricklayers' Hall is the headquarters of one of Dublin's oldest Guilds – the Incorporated Brick and Stonelayers' Trade Unions. Its members helped to build the Custom House. Indeed, they had a strike, then, in protest against masons being brought from England.

Bricklayers' Hall will not disappear from Cuffe Street. It was dismantled stone by stone, and every stone numbered. The whole building is being moved farther back on the site.

Cuffe Street seems much shorter now than it did in childhood days. So Stephen's Green is sooner reached. St. Stephen's Green has always been St. Stephen's Green ever since man gave names to bits of countryside. The name seemed right for a patch of land standing near

to the leper hospital of St. Stephen. It was not changed when the leper hospital had gone and Mary Mercer built her hospital on the site. And it is unlikely to change even though now, unfortunately, Mercer's has been closed, and the building taken over by the College of Surgeons.

The patch began to take its familiar shape as the land around was developed as a residential area. The Fitzgeralds began the move by building Kildare House, the front facing the city, the no less ornate back looking onto still untouched land that was to become Merrion Square and provide No. 1 Merrion Square as a house for Dr. and Mrs. Wilde and their son Oscar.

Dublin society followed the Fitzgeralds, and bought its lots and built its villas in what became one of the largest squares in Europe. The centre of the square was reserved as common land.

Eventually, the Guinness family bought two of the houses, and converted them into Iveagh House. And Lord Ardilaun, in 1880, paid £20,000 to have St. Stephen's Green laid out as a park for the citizens of Dublin.

Street names that are common now began to be familiar. Dawson Street. Kildare Street. And what had, for long enough, been a laneway from Dame Street to the Green was developed as Grafton Street, and soon had household names along its fashionable thoroughfare. Brown Thomas and Co., whose facade still carries announcements about its business. Jewellers like Weirs. When Mr. Whyte closed his school, Bewleys opened their Oriental Cafe. And Switzers opened on the corner of Wicklow Street.

They are still there. And the crowds. Safer, now that the street has been pedestrianised, and the Gardai have no fear they'll be asked to stop a runaway bull like Constable Sheehan had to do in 1904.

Eighteen stone and six foot four the Constable was, and brave by nature. His bravery killed him. At twenty-nine, he was killed trying to rescue John Fleming from a gas-filled sewer in 1905. Dublin set up a memorial to his bravery on Burgh Quay.

The west side of the Green was slow to develop. A graveyard and an execution site were part of the reason. The main reason, though, seems to have been that it was subject to raids from thieves and robbers from the area nearby.

The College of Surgeons was built in 1809. On the site of an old graveyard, and near the spot where, in 1729, young Mary Creighton had been executed for stealing a calico dress.

Joshua Dawson opened up Dawson Street and built his house there, which he later sold to Dublin Corporation as the Lord Mayor's House.

Michael Burke bought Kerry House, the home of the

Marquis of Lansdowne, and turned it into the Shelbourne Hotel, the place where, in 1922, the Constitution of the Irish Free State was drafted. The Fitzgerald's house was bought by the Royal Dublin Society, and later became Leinster House, the seat of Dáil Eireann. The RDS moved out to Ballsbridge.

Francis Higgins, the "Sham Squire," lived at number 81. He inveigled his way into society, and made a career of spying. He informed on Lord Edward Fitzgerald. So hated was he that, when he died and was buried at Kilbarrack Church on the coast road to Howth, his grave had to be guarded lest it be desecrated.

Down the way from Iveagh House is Newman House, where John Henry Newman was Rector of the newly founded Catholic University, which was later incorporated into University College Dublin when it was built in Earlsford Terrace. Newman House was originally the home of Buck Whaley. A notorious gambler, Whaley once made a bet that he would walk to Jerusalem, play ball against the walls, and return to Dublin within a year. The undertaking cost him £8,000. But he won the bet, and made a profit of £7,000. The Guinness family presented Iveagh House to the nation in 1939. Nowadays it's used for receptions by the Department of Foreign Affairs.

History and the developers changed the face of things outside the Green, but inside, except for an additional statue here and there, things are much the same as they were in Dublin long ago.

Still neat, clean and lovingly cared for. A personal place that has its own meaning for everybody.

Two children race along the path, through the reds and whites and greens of regimented flowers, to the water fountain glistening in the sun. They know that if they stand where the water wets the parapet, they'll feel the spray on their faces.

Half Dublin idles round the bandstand, watching the Ballyboden Majorettes.

A man walks lonely with his red setter dog, and hardly hears the child noise from the swings and see-saws in the play park.

Three pigeons by the lakeside tidy away the crumbs the ducks have left untouched. A mother wheels a push-chair by, assuring the child that if it's fine again tomorrow, they'll come and feed the ducks.

A young man paces smartly home, his new "Fresh Coffee Maker" showing through a Bewley's yellow bag.

A blind man sits by the scented shrubbery. Tom Kettle and the Countess Markievicz in their memorials keep him silent company.

Round the corner, by the bridge, Tom Pat fishes, his catch of seven pinkeens already in the jar. And pleasure blushes his face, shadowed by a shock of fair hair that puts the finishing touches to the picture of an angel. He's

played round the giant memorial to Yeats that's hidden by the trees. But it's early days for a Dublin lad to give his mind to Ben Bulbin, or even to Joyce, whose memorial keeps a critical eye on the Catholic University Church on the far side of the Green. He's still too young to understand who the Fates are or what they're about. His mother, though, looks the sort of woman who'd let him stop on the way out to Leeson Park to admire the bronze the Germans gave to the nation in gratitude for helping their recovery after World War II.

There are enough gates to get out of the Green. The most impressive one looks like the Arc de Triomphe in Paris. It is Dublin's memorial to the Royal Dublin Fusiliers who fought and were killed in the Boer War. The name of every man is inscribed in the arch.

The gate leads out to South King Street and Grafton Street. South King Street means the Gaiety Theatre, where for years Jimmy O'Dea reigned as Dublin's king of comedy. Nowadays Maureen Potter wears the crown. And Dubliners are "ony delira."

Grafton Street, busy, bustling, bright with buskers and street artists, leads to Trinity College. With some reminders on the way that Michael Balfe, who wrote "The Bohemian Girl", was born in Balfe Street when it was called Pitt street, and Wolfe Tone married Matilda Witherington who lived in Chatham Street.

The wall of Trinity College runs the length of one side of Nassau Street. The other side is shops. Hanna's book shop at one end, Greene's at the other. Between them they've served the world of books and book-readers for generations. And halfway along, that marvellous invention as an outlet for Irish craft, the Kilkenny Design Centre.

Just looking at Trinity College is a pleasure. The eighteenth century architects did Dublin a good turn when they took on the task of replacing the buildings that first housed the university.

Elizabeth I granted the charter in 1591, and "the College of the Holy and Undivided Trinity of Queen Elizabeth, near Dublin," was built on the site of All Hallows Priory. It goes without saying that Trinity is an academic institution, and has provided the nation and the world with men and women of intellectual power.

That said, however, it still remains that Trinity College is famous because it is the home of the Book of Kells, the illuminated version of the Four Gospels.

The manuscript is on public view in the old Library. And the Library itself is worth looking at.

Even getting from the front gate to the Library is a pleasure that will be often recollected... The first sight of the Campanile through the entrance arch, the walk across the cobblestones in Parliament Square. The Chapel. The Dining Hall sadly burnt in 1984, but now restored. To cut around by the new Arts Building, and walk in College Park. Or maybe just sit when the evening sun casts gentle shadows.

It's an atmosphere is Trinity. And just visiting there is an education.

Out of Trinity and across College Green is Westmoreland Street. The street once meant The Irish Times and press photos in the window. But they moved from the front of the building and now work in D'Olier Street. Even the clock is gone. To D'Olier Street as well.

At the end of the street is O'Connell Bridge.

Stand on the bridge where you can look up and down the river. Up to the west is the Metal Bridge. The loveliest bridge on the river. It's also known as the Ha'penny Bridge from the days when there was a toll to cross it. It stands opposite the Merchants Arch, which must be the most used thoroughfare in Dublin. Nowadays it leads to a maze of streets behind the Central Bank that are coming into their own again. In their own way they give a feeling of what Dublin used to be.

Down to the east, towards the mouth of the river, is Butt Bridge. Just beyond the bridge is the Custom House that Gandon built. But it is hard to appreciate it from here. The view is ruined by a railway loopline. Look at it downriver from the south bank.

Butt Bridge used to be the last bridge on the Liffey. Now there are two more.

One of them is Matt Talbot Bridge. Motorists take their life in their hands every time they cross it. It has to be the craziest traffic system in the world.

Beyond that is the recently added East Link Bridge. And as the man said, "If they build any more bridges, we'll see the Liffey only through the chinks in the tunnel."

The East Link is a toll bridge. But worth the money, for it leads to the lovely coastal route by Ringsend and Sandymount and Booterstown. James Joyce country. And then on through Blackrock to Dunlaoghaire and Sandycove and the Joyce Museum.

James Joyce grew up in the days when the O'Connell Bridge you're standing on was Carlisle Bridge, and O'Connell Street was Sackville Street, and Drogheda Street before that. But that was before Dan O'Connell's monument was erected. The General Post Office dominates O'Connell Street. It nearly didn't. In the 1800s there were plans to build the Roman Catholic Cathedral there. The religious bigotry of the day prevented that, and the Pro-Cathedral was built, instead, off the main thoroughfare in Marlborough Street.

Radio Eireann began broadcasting on the top floor of the GPO. The entrance was a quiet little door in Henry Street.

Now Radio Telefís Eireann operates from Donnybrook, in a setting that is the envy of many a television corporation. And they have an almost permanent waiting list for television's longest-running chat programme, The Late Late Show with Gay Byrne.

Eason's is on this side of the GPO. It's noticeable now. But when it began a hundred years ago, it was a small bookstall in Sackville Street. Look at it now!

Clery's is on the opposite side of the street. And has been there, a landmark and something of an institution in shopping, for over a century.

But admire the GPO for, having been built in 1818, it was nearly destroyed in the 1916 Rising.

Round the corner from the General Post Office, and a right turn off Henry Street is Moore Street.

Henry Street is special, but Moore Street is Dublin. Dirty, noisy, boisterous, crowded, colourful, witty, sad and happy all at once. Fish, vegetables, fruit, green, red and yellow, in pyramids on stalls that stand more by magic than careful engineering. Bread shops that seem stocked for a famine. Meat shops that give the impression that every pig, cow and sheep in the country has just been slaughtered. And bazaars where you'll buy whether you need it or not... But nobody can tell you about Moore Street. It's a personal experience.

Once upon a time Nelson's Pillar towered over everything in O'Connell Street.

Not any more. Someone blew him up. In the dead of night, at 1.32 a.m. on Tuesday, March 8, 1966. And shook Dublin and blew out the windows in O'Connell Street in the process.

Only the pedestal was left. And the problem of how to deal with it.

The Army Engineers. Quietly they laid a ditch of sand down the middle of the street, set their explosives, and at 3.30 precisely on a spring morning, pressed the button. The pedestal crumpled and fell like an oak falls in the forest.

One window in O'Connell Street, they say, was broken. The one they forgot to open in Radio Eireann on the top floor of the GPO.

But Nelson is not altogether gone. They found his head. It reposes in the Civic Museum in South William Street, still keeping his good eye on the place.

A bit down from O'Connell Bridge, in a turn left off Eden Quay, is the Abbey Theatre. And home of W.B. Yeats and Lady Gregory. Not to mention Hugh Leonard and J.B. Keane.

And what about Sean O'Casey? A Dublin man bred and born who shaped the city and its people into words.

Don't stir from where you are, and every character he ever wrote about will pass you as you're standing there.

They haven't changed.

Not in a thousand years.

Facing page: Dublin's elegant Georgian doorways.

An imposing statue of Daniel O'Connell (above), by sculptor John Henry Foley, dominates the southern end of O'Connell Street, Dublin's principal thoroughfare and one of the broadest streets in Europe. In the 1740s Luke Gardiner, whose family did much to beautify the city, widened the street to 150 feet and planted the mall with trees, and it became one of the first areas to constitute the fashionable north Dublin of the 18th century. Facing page: the splendid Renaissance-style building in Kildare Street that became the home of the National Library in 1890, (right) Heuston Station, a striking building designed by SanctonWood and dating from the mid-1840s, and (above right) Leinster House, which was built in 1745 and is one of the finest of Dublin's Georgian mansions. Originally the town house of the Dukes of Leinster, it became Government property in the early 1900s, providing accommodation for the two houses of the Republic of Ireland Parliament.

Standing in elegant Merrion Square is an institution of which Dubliners are particularly proud, the National Gallery of Ireland (these pages). It was opened in 1864 largely due to the efforts of William Dargan, the prime instigator of the Exhibition of 1853. A statue of him stands outside the building (below), as does a statue of George Bernard Shaw (facing page bottom left), who maintained that he owed his education to the gallery and left a third of his estate to it. Designed by Francis Fowke, the gallery has some fine rooms in which is housed a remarkable collection including works from all major European schools and a comprehensive selection from Irish artists. Overleaf: the decorative stairwells of (left) the National Gallery and (right) City Hall.

Built by Francis Johnston in 1815-18, the General Post Office (above), on O'Connell Street, is an impressive building and is also of historic interest, having been the headquarters of the Irish Volunteers during the Insurrection of 1916. Its interior was badly damaged by shells but has since been restored to its original splendour and features a plaque (right) bearing the declaration of the patriots. Facing page: the Four Courts (top), overlooking the River Liffey, has housed Dublin's Courts of Law since 1796, when they were moved there from the precincts of Christ Church Cathedral. The six Corinthian columns of the portico are surmounted by a statue of Moses, with Justice and Mercy on either side. The Bank of Ireland (bottom), one of the finest Georgian buildings in the city, was begun by Edward Lovett Pearce in 1729. Statues depicting Hibernia, Fidelity and Commerce stand above the elegant Ionic portico.

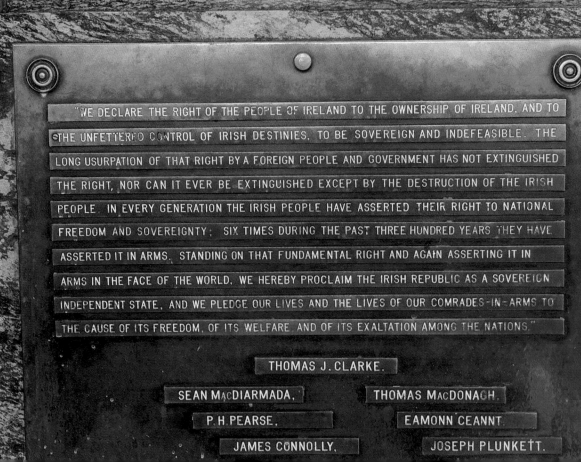

"WE DECLARE THE RIGHT OF THE PEOPLE OF IRELAND TO THE OWNERSHIP OF IRELAND, AND TO THE UNFETTERED CONTROL OF IRISH DESTINIES, TO BE SOVEREIGN AND INDEFEASIBLE. THE LONG USURPATION OF THAT RIGHT BY A FOREIGN PEOPLE AND GOVERNMENT HAS NOT EXTINGUISHED THE RIGHT, NOR CAN IT EVER BE EXTINGUISHED EXCEPT BY THE DESTRUCTION OF THE IRISH PEOPLE. IN EVERY GENERATION THE IRISH PEOPLE HAVE ASSERTED THEIR RIGHT TO NATIONAL FREEDOM AND SOVEREIGNTY; SIX TIMES DURING THE PAST THREE HUNDRED YEARS THEY HAVE ASSERTED IT IN ARMS. STANDING ON THAT FUNDAMENTAL RIGHT AND AGAIN ASSERTING IT IN ARMS IN THE FACE OF THE WORLD, WE HEREBY PROCLAIM THE IRISH REPUBLIC AS A SOVEREIGN INDEPENDENT STATE, AND WE PLEDGE OUR LIVES AND THE LIVES OF OUR COMRADES-IN-ARMS TO THE CAUSE OF ITS FREEDOM, OF ITS WELFARE, AND OF ITS EXALTATION AMONG THE NATIONS."

THOMAS J. CLARKE.

SEAN MacDIARMADA,　　　THOMAS MacDONAGH.

P. H. PEARSE,　　　EAMONN CEANNT.

JAMES CONNOLLY,　　　JOSEPH PLUNKETT.

Previous pages: a view of the River Liffey at sunset. Rising near Sally Gap in the Wicklow Hills, the river describes almost a full circle as it flows eastwards into Dublin's harbour, emptying into the sea at Dublin Bay. Marsh's Library (these pages), on the east side of St Patrick's Cathedral, was built by Archbishop Narcissus Marsh in 1707 and is the oldest of Ireland's public libraries. Its darkened oak shelves contain some 25,000 beautifully-bound volumes - chiefly of medicine, theology and ancient literature - and its treasures include Dean Swift's copy of Clarendon's "History of the Great Rebellion" with his own pencilled annotations. Overleaf: a view of broad O'Connell Street from the south side of O'Connell Bridge.

Facing page: (top) elegant Georgian houses on Merrion Square, and (bottom) Leinster House and the cenotaph to Arthur Griffith and Michael Collins. Right; a statue of Robert Emmet on St Stephen's Green (this page), where many Dubliners choose to relax.

Previous pages: the early morning sun gilds modern Liberty Hall and the Metal Footbridge - or Halfpenny Bridge - spanning the River Liffey, while the domed Custom House looms on the horizon. Facing page bottom: the same scene under the day's blue sky. Facing page top: Queen Maev Bridge leading to Arran Quay, which is dominated by the tower of St Paul's Church, dating from 1835-40. Beyond is the green dome of the Four Courts, which rises above the jostling roofs of quayside houses (below). O'Connell Bridge (right) leads into O'Connell Street and was first named Carlisle Bridge when it was built in 1794. In 1880 it was renamed, flattened and widened, making it rather remarkable in that it is now broader than it is long. The magnificent reading room (overleaf) in the National Library was opened in 1890 to house the collections of the Royal Dublin Society, previously housed at Leinster House.

Christ Church Cathedral (these pages) is Dublin's oldest building, having been founded by Donat, first Bishop of Dublin, and the Norse King Sitric of Dublin in about 1038. In 1172 construction was renewed on a greater scale with the help of sponsorship from Strongbow and St Laurence O'Toole. Its splendid interior contains some fascinating treasures, including an effigy of Strongbow (below right), supposedly marking his burial place, with another alongside said to be either that of his wife or of his son, whom according to legend he cut in two for being a coward. Exquisite chandeliers light the sumptuous Drawing Room (overleaf) of the State Apartments in Dublin Castle. Originally a Norse stronghold dating from 1208 to 1220, the castle proper was built during the reign of King John, eventually becoming the residence of the lord deputy, or viceroy.

This page: views of the River Liffey at dusk, spanned by O'Connell Bridge (facing page top), Queen Maev Bridge (right) and the famous Metal Footbridge (remaining pictures), which was built in 1816 and is also known as Halfpenny Bridge due to the toll charged in the early 1900s. Flowing from the west to Dublin Bay in the east, the River Liffey cuts through the very heart of Dublin, and a walk along its banks can be a good way to become acquainted with aspects of the city's character. Lining the busy quays are to be found warehouses, the variously-painted facades of tenement buildings and auction rooms full of odds and ends, as well as some of the city's finest buildings, one of which is the Custom House (overleaf right). Overleaf left: the rectangular layout of Dublin's Trinity College beside the semi-circular facade of the Bank of Ireland.

The friendliness of Dublin's vendors makes shopping there a very pleasurable experience, especially at lively markets such as those in St Thomas Street (above and facing page bottom) and St Michans's Street (right and top pictures). Facing page top: shops on Meath Street.

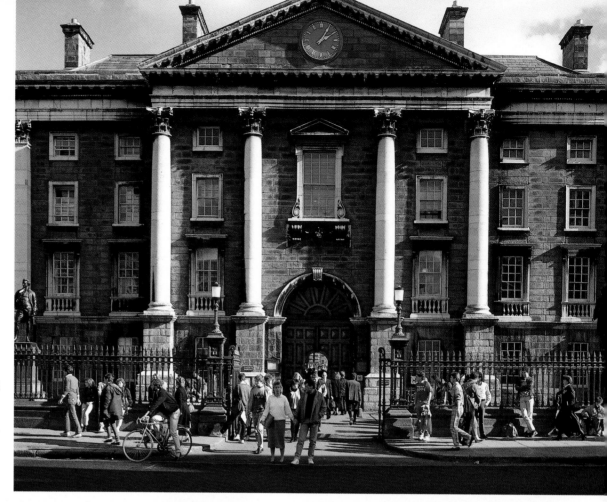

Apart from its merit as an educational establishment, Trinity College (these pages) has a long and prestigious history, having been founded by Elizabeth I in 1591. Being situated at the centre of Ireland's capital it has played a greater role in the country's affairs than is usual for a university, and has often been a forum for heated political debate. An impressive number of great minds have flourished in its lively atmosphere - Congreve, Bishop Berkeley, Swift, Emmet and Wilde to name but a few. The college's spacious quadrangle is dominated by the Campanile (below and facing page bottom), which was built by Sir Charles Lanyon in 1853, while its grand, Palladian-style West Front (remaining pictures) was built between 1752 and 1759. Overleaf: O'Connell Street and O'Connell Bridge.

Facing page: animals at Dublin Zoo, which was established in 1830 and is the world's third oldest public zoo. It is among the many attractions in Phoenix Park (remaining pictures), which, covering around 2,000 acres, is one of Europe's largest parks.

Previous pages: Government Buildings, formerly the Science Buildings of University College, designed by Sir Aston Webb, R.A. and built in 1904-10, and (right) the President of Ireland's residence, built in the 1750s by Nathaniel Clements and set in the green expanse of Phoenix Park. Above: yachts and the E.S.B. Power Station on Dublin Harbour, (facing page bottom) Halfpenny Bridge, and (facing page top) the *Lady Patricia* docked at City Quay near the Talbot Memorial Bridge, beyond which rise the very contrasting outlines of the Custom House and Liberty Hall (right). The former, built between 1781 and 1791 by James Gandon, has a most impressive facade, best seen from across the river, and a 38-metre-high copper dome topped by a statue of Commerce. The designers of Liberty Hall did not attempt to match such Georgian splendour and, in 1960, erected a building of elegant simplicity that functions as the headquarters of the Irish Transport and General Workers Union.

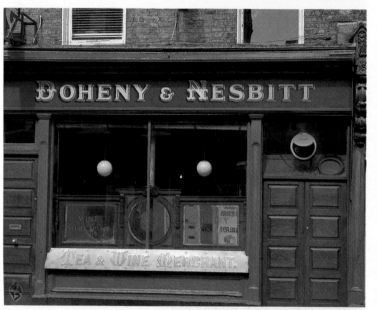

The village of Malahide, a resort on the coast north of Dublin, is distinguished by its fine castle (previous pages), the residence of the Talbot de Malahide family from 1185 to 1976. Set in 265 acres of land, it comprises buildings from several periods, including the 12th-century, three storey tower house and two drum-like towers dating from around 1765. Among the treasures within the castle is a fine collection of portraits forming the nucleus of the National Gallery's National Portrait Collection. It includes a number of portrayals of people and events relevant to the castle's and Ireland's history. Along with many fine Georgian buildings the streets of central Dublin are enhanced by the traditional facades of its shops, pubs and theatres (these pages), whose colourful paintwork and ornate signs bring to mind an age gone by. Left: the Olympia Theatre on Dame Street, and (below) the Brazen Head Hotel, which has a bar that is reputedly the city's oldest, dating from 1666.

Situated near the main southeast gate of Phoenix Park is a striking, 205-foot-high obelisk, the Wellington Testimonial (facing page), which was erected two years after Waterloo, in 1817. Designed by Sir William Smirke, its pedestal is decorated with bronze panels depicting Wellington's battles in bas relief. On the south bank of the River Liffey, near Kilmainham, is Memorial Park (right), which was laid out by Lutyens and commemorates the First World War. Below: the smooth waters of the Liffey under a golden sky, dominated by the Wellington Testimonial.

The National Museum was designed in Renaissance style by Sir Thomas Deane and opened in 1890. Its exquisitely decorated interior (previous pages) contains a large collection of Irish antiquities dating from the Stone Age period onwards. Some of the most beautiful of its priceless exhibits are the gold pieces of jewellery from the Bronze Age, while other items include the Ardagh Chalice and the Tara Brooch, both dating from the eighth century. Above: the grand entrance to Government Buildings, formerly the Science Buildings of University College, and (left) the Campanile in the quadrangle of Trinity College, which is also the site of the 'Long Room' (facing page). This beautiful library measures 209 feet in length and houses some of the finest Celtic manuscripts in the world, including the Book of Durrow and the Book of Kells.

Left: the covered market off Great George's Street, (below and bottom left) Greene's Bookshop in Clare Street, (bottom) Merchant's Alley, and (facing page) the Parnell Monument at the northern end of O'Connell Street. Overleaf: Parnell Street.

Facing page: (top) the Nissan Bicycle Race and (bottom) the Dublin Marathon. Top: the Four Courts, overlooking the River Liffey, and (above) the interior and (right) gate of the Tailors Hall, which dates from 1796 and is the city's only remaining guild hall.

According to tradition, St Patrick's Cathedral (these pages) stands where the saint himself baptised converts in a well that appeared when he struck the ground with his staff. The original church dates from 1192 yet the present magnificent edifice - at 300 feet, the longest church in Ireland - is largely the result of restoration carried out in the 19th century. Of particular interest is the church's association with the celebrated, and bitter, satirist Jonathan Swift, who was Dean of St Patrick's from 1713 to 1745. He is buried in the south aisle, where - according to the epitaph he wrote himself - "savage indignation can no longer rend his heart". The Four Courts (overleaf), on the north bank of the River Liffey, was built between 1786 and 1802 by the great architect, James Gandon. It contains the original courts of Exchequer, Common Pleas, King's Bench and Chancery.

Facing page: fruit and vegetable stalls on Moore Street, and colourful
flowers on sale at the market (top) in the arcade between Great George's
Street and Drury Street and (above and left) in Grafton Street.
Overleaf: the O'Connell Monument on O'Connell Street.

Left: the formidable gates of Kilmainham Jail (remaining pictures), which dates from 1792 and has lodged such famous Irish patriots as Parnell, Davitt and Robert Emmet. It was also the execution place of many Volunteer leaders, including Patrick Pearse and James Connolly, and is now open as a museum.

When it was begun in 1729 the
Bank of Ireland (above) was
intended to house the Irish
Parliament. It was, however, made
redundant in 1800 when the
British and Irish parliaments
united in London under the Act of
Union. When the building was
sold, for the sum of £40,000, it was
stipulated that the interior should
be redesigned so as to exclude its
use as a public debating forum.
The only room to retain its
original appearance is the Old
House of Lords (right), in which is
hung a splendid 1,233-piece,
Waterford crystal chandelier and
two great tapestries woven by Jan
van Beaver depicting the Battle of
the Boyne and the Siege of Derry.
Facing page: (top) O'Connell
Bridge, and (bottom) Heuston
Bridge and Station. Overleaf:
aerial views of central Dublin,
picturing (left) the curving facade
of the Bank of Ireland and
Westmoreland Street leading over
the Liffey into O'Connell Street,
and (right) the domed Four Courts,
the square tower of Christ Church
Cathedral and the quadrangle and
crenellated Record Tower of
Dublin Castle.

One of Dublin's most prized assets is Phoenix Park (these pages), which first belonged to the priory of the Knights of St John, was seized by Henry VIII at the Reformation and opened to the public in the mid-1700s by the viceroy, Lord Chesterfield. Amongst its many interesting sights is the towering cross of steel (facing page) that stands where Pope John Paul II celebrated mass during his visit in 1979. Overleaf: the market on Moore Street.

Top: the control room, (top left and left) the exhibition at the Malt House, and (above) the gates, of the Guinness Brewery (facing page), where the famed Dublin stout has been made since 1759. Overleaf: the Royal Hospital in Kilmainham, with its ornate chapel (right).

Top and left: the fine building that was once the Canal Hotel, at Portobello Lock and Canal (above). Facing page: (top) the Mansion House, where the lord mayors of Dublin have lived since 1715, and (bottom) Leinster House, built in 1745.

One of the most macabre of the city's historic sights is the group of mummified bodies (previous pages left) in the crypt of St Michan's Church. It is likely that their extraordinary preservation is due to the moisture-absorbing power of the church's limestone walls, although a more imaginative explanation attributes it to the embalming spirit released in an explosion at a nearby distillery. St Michan's is one of Dublin's oldest churches, having been founded in 1095, though much of the present edifice is the result of 17th-century rebuilding and 19th-century restoration. Among its many points of interest is the old organ in the main aisle (previous pages, right) that was reputedly played by Handel. Right: St Audoen's Church, which is the city's earliest existing parish church, dating mainly from the 12th century, (below) the Royal Hospital, founded by Charles II and built in 1680 - 84 for veteran and disabled soldiers, and (below right) a memorial stone backed by Collins Barracks, formerly the Royal Barracks of 1704. Facing page: a lock on the Grand Canal.

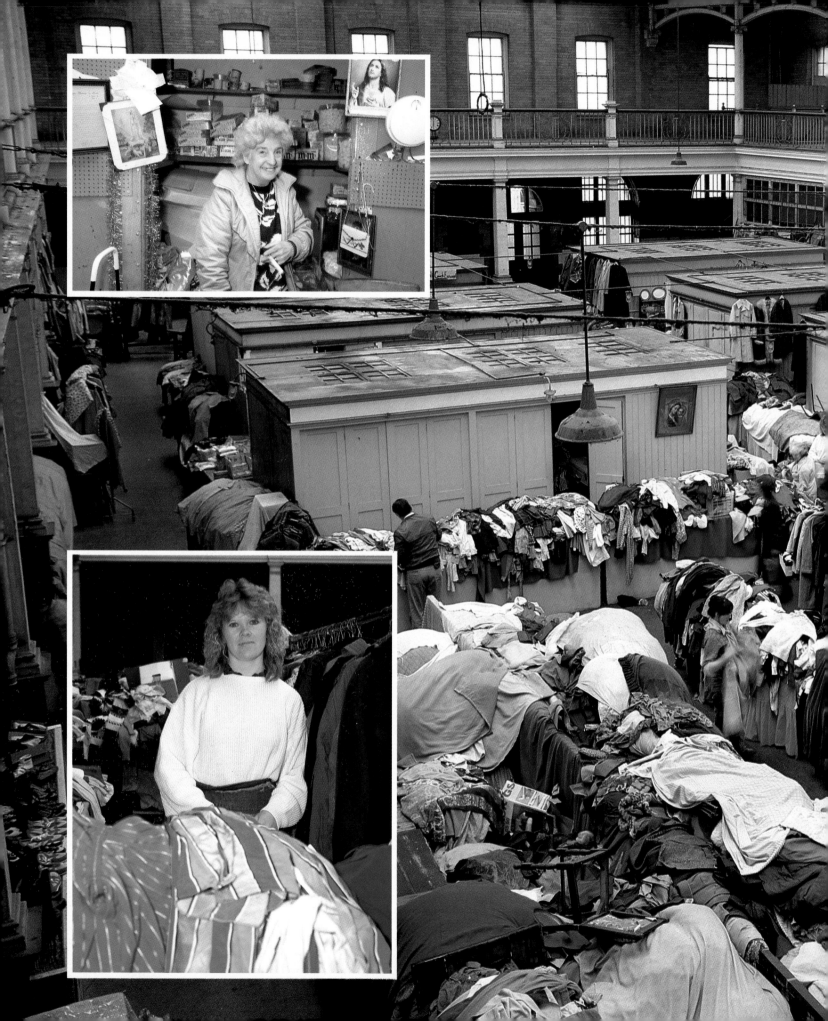

Previous pages: colourful clothes and bric-a-brac in Iveagh Markets, in Francis St. Located within easy reach of the city centre are a variety of picturesque and interesting places to visit. Running parallel to the northern shores of Dublin Bay is the three-mile-long sandbank, North Bull Island, which in days gone by was the cause of countless shipwrecks, providing local residents with great quantities of booty. Today, the island's attractions include long stretches of golden beach (facing page bottom), a bird sanctuary and two golf courses. Further east, crowning the bay's northern arm, is beautiful Howth Head (remaining pictures). A splendid 15th-century castle can be seen from the road leading to charming Howth Village, which is known for its beautiful gardens and great, sheltered harbour (facing page top). The latter, built in 1807-9, is used as a fishing port as well as a mooring place for pleasure craft (right). From 19th-century Bailey Lighthouse (above), on the southern shores of Howth Head, the Wicklow Hills are visible. Overleaf: Halfpenny Bridge and the lights of Dublin reflected in the River Liffey.